RESILIENCE
BREAKING THE CHAINS

RESILIENCE
BREAKING THE CHAINS

EUGENE Z. BERTRAND

Halo
PUBLISHING
INTERNATIONAL

To those who have endured pain behind closed doors
and found the strength to break free.

To the survivors, the healers, and the ones
who never stopped believing in a better tomorrow.

Even in your darkest moments,
love and resilience will always light the way.

This is for you.

To my family and friends, whose patience, love, and belief
in this story held me up when self-doubt set in, thank you
for being my shelter and my compass.

To my little brother, Eli, I am writing this book in part
to show you that if you set your mind to something, there
is nothing in this world you will not be able to achieve,
no matter what obstacles come your way. Your resilience
inspires me and reminds me that what seems
impossible is often within our reach.

CONTENTS

AUTHOR'S NOTE

This story is one that speaks to the courage it takes to walk away from the past, the struggle of rebuilding a sense of trust, and the hope that comes with new beginnings.

For anyone who has ever felt trapped in a situation they could not control, for those who have faced their worst fears and somehow come out the other side, this book is for you. It is a reminder that even the hardest puzzles have a solution. Even when we are at our most vulnerable, there is strength.

This is a journey of survival—learning to love and trust again, and, ultimately, reclaiming the once-lost peace. The road to healing is long, but as you will see, it is also one worth traveling.

With this story, I hope to offer not just a narrative of struggle but one of resilience. May you find in these pages the courage to face your own challenges and the hope to believe that healing is always possible, no matter what has happened.

In life, we often hear about the power of family—the unbreakable bonds, the unconditional love, and the safety and comfort that come with it. But what happens when the very people meant to protect us become the source of our deepest pain? This story is one of resilience and survival— the quiet, often messy path toward healing after enduring unimaginable betrayal within the home.

This book is not just about the trauma or the pain, but about finding strength in the aftermath. It is about how the human spirit can endure, even when it feels as if the world were crumbling around us.

To my readers, especially those walking the long road toward healing, I hope these pages offer you comfort, solidarity, and renewed hope. You are not alone.

Finally, for every survivor still searching for their voice, this book is for you.

May you know your story matters.

Chapter 1

THE FIRST SIGNS
REALIZING THE QUIET SHIFT

*Nathan Parker had never known a single day
without his mother's steady presence.*

Nathan Parker had never known a single day without his mother's steady presence. Angela wasn't just his foundation; she was the ground beneath his feet, the quiet force that made the world feel safe. Fiercely protective, unwavering, and strong in ways he didn't fully understand, she gave him the sense that nothing could touch them. Even on the hardest days, her hand on his shoulder or the certainty in her voice was enough to make him believe they could weather anything. Nathan was the only child of his mother, Angela, and his biological father, Kacey. They divorced right before Nathan could tie his own shoes; Nathan dared not speak of it.

Their home in a small town outside of Boston had always felt like a safe haven, filled with quiet traditions, music from old records, and the comforting scent of his mother's cinnamon tea. Nathan remembered evenings when he and Angela played cards at the kitchen table, laughing at their own bad hands, the air light and easy for that brief time.

Angela, a psychotherapist, always had a warm smile and clear eyes; she listened quietly when others spoke, her head slightly tilted, a small line of concentration between her brows. She single-handedly raised Nathan. But when she first met Richard, there was a flicker of something she hadn't expected, a cautious hope she barely allowed herself to feel. *Don't get carried away, Angie; this might not even work out,* she'd told herself, tucking it deep inside before anyone could see.

Everything shifted when Richard Armstrong appeared, first as a friendly stranger with smooth charm and kind eyes, then quickly as someone who seemed to slot effortlessly into their lives. At the school's spring fundraiser, Richard handed out cupcakes he'd baked himself, joking about his "disaster" in the kitchen, making Nathan's school principal laugh so hard she had to wipe her eyes. He greeted Nathan's band-mates by name, complimented neighbors' roses, and even asked after the local librarian's sick husband.

To the crowd, he was magnetic. Oftentimes, even Nathan found himself smiling. To everyone else, Richard was magnetic. Even Nathan, as wary as he was, had wanted to believe in that version of Richard…at least at first. He had a disarming charm that wrapped around people like velvet. To Nathan, however, he was a shadow learning how to wear light.

He was a businessman who often went on trips and knew how to make people feel important. At first, Nathan admired him; it was nice seeing his mom happy again after years of focusing solely on raising him. At family gatherings, Richard always had a joke ready, laughing with neighbors as if he belonged in every crowd. Nathan watched how people leaned in when Richard spoke, trusting him without question.

To neighbors, Richard was the perfect gentleman. Always ready to greet someone with a warm handshake, a harmless joke, or a quick offer to help carry groceries. Once, Nathan overheard their neighbor, Mrs. Delaney, laugh about how "Richard's the kind you can trust with a spare key." That was the trick. He made trust look easy. He volunteered at local events in the community, attended church from time to time, donated to the school fundraiser, and never forgot to ask how someone's kids were doing.

When the door clicked shut, however, Richard's warmth vanished like a candle snuffed in a gust. He didn't need to raise his voice; he curated discomfort like an artist... carefully, deliberately.

However, as the months went by, Richard's presence began to shift the balance in their home. He became more controlling. It started with little things, always deciding what they should eat for dinner and insisting on how things should be arranged in the house. Over time, Nathan began to notice that his mother became quieter around Richard, but constantly tried to please him.

Nathan watched his mother's eyes dart toward Richard before she spoke, the weight of unspoken fears pressing down as her words faltered and fell away. Each hesitant breath, each swallowed sentence gnawed at something deep inside him. This wasn't simply awkwardness; it was almost as if shadows were creeping into the light, a silent warning Nathan couldn't yet name.

By the time Richard and Angela got married, Nathan was about sixteen years old. From birth, Nathan had always had a great relationship with his mother, but after the wedding, it felt as if an invisible wall had gone up between them.

Richard never raised his voice; he didn't have to. His silence could slice deeper than any scream; it was heavy and deliberate, like a slowly tightening noose. And when he smiled, it wasn't warmth you felt; it was a warning, a quiet mockery that left you questioning your own sanity for ever thinking something was wrong.

One Saturday afternoon, Nathan wandered into the kitchen in search of a snack, the kind of lazy weekend moment that should have felt ordinary. But the second he stepped through the doorway, he saw Richard, already there, leaning against the counter as if he owned the room. A half-empty mug of coffee rested in his hand, steam curling lazily toward the ceiling. From the living room, the television's faint mutters, but in the kitchen, the air felt unnaturally still, as if even the walls were holding their breath.

Richard didn't say anything at first. His eyes tracked Nathan's every move as he crossed to the fridge. The hint of a smile tugged at his lips, polite enough to look harmless, yet sharp enough to feel like a warning. It was the kind of smile that made you question whether you'd done something wrong before you even had a chance to speak.

"You need to be more responsible now that I am in the picture, young man," Richard finally said with a slight smile, but there was an edge to his words. "No more of this childish behavior. You are almost a damn adult; grow the hell up. If you can't, there's the door; you can leave." The pause after that sentence felt loaded, as if it were a trap baited with expectation.

Nathan did not know how to respond. He was not a troublemaker by any means. He got decent grades, played guitar in a local band, and spent most of his free time hanging out with his close group of friends. But nothing he did seemed to satisfy Richard.

The rest of the day moved in fragments, Nathan drifting from room to room, carrying the weight of Richard's words like stones in his pockets. He avoided the kitchen after that, retreating into the quieter corners of the house where the air felt less sharp. But no matter where he went, the echo of that faint smile and those loaded pauses followed him, a shadow he couldn't shake.

By evening, the sky had turned the color of slate, and the first low rumbles of thunder began to crawl across the horizon. That evening, there was a storm that rattled the windows, wind whistling through the cracks as if the house itself were holding its breath. Nathan sat on the couch with his shoulders rounded, his knees drawn in slightly, as though trying to take up less space. His hands were clasped so tightly his knuckles ached.

"Mom…there's something you never knew," he said, his voice thin and brittle.

Angela's stomach sank. "What is it?"

He stared at the floor. "When I was little, Dad would lock me in my room for hours. Sometimes all day. He wouldn't let me eat. I'd lie on the floor staring at the light under the door, just hoping it would move, that someone would come." His throat bobbed. "It wasn't punishment… It was just because he could."

Angela's breath faltered. She opened her mouth, but before she could speak, the front door creaked open.

Richard stepped inside, shaking water from his coat, his eyes flicking from Nathan to Angela. He had lingered just long enough to listen before interjecting. The air seemed to tighten around them. "What's going on here?" His voice was measured, but there was a thread beneath it that warned of something sharper.

Nathan swallowed, feeling the old fear creep in. "I was telling Mom something. Something that Dad used to do to. Not a big deal…no worries, Richard."

Richard closed the door with a soft click, hung his coat with slow precision, then stepped into the room. He didn't sit—he loomed just enough to cast a shadow over Nathan. "You understand," he said evenly, "that these are serious things you're saying. Things that can't be unsaid. And if they're not true…" He let the words trail off, heavy with threat.

"They *are* true," Nathan said, but the conviction he'd had moments ago was thinning fast.

Richard's gaze locked on him, cool and unblinking. "I didn't have to be there to know, Nathan. You were a difficult child sometimes. You know that. You had trouble listening, trouble following rules. It wasn't easy for anyone."

He shifted his attention to Angela, his voice softening. "Kids remember moments differently. They remember the parts that hurt, not the parts that led up to them."

Nathan's stomach twisted. The implication was there, sharp and poisonous—"You brought it on yourself."

Richard crouched slightly so his face was closer to Nathan's. "If you leave out details, it changes the story. And then good people get hurt because someone wanted to settle a score."

Nathan's chest tightened until breathing hurt. "That's not—"

Richard's hand came down on his shoulder, not hard, but firm enough to make the rest of the words stick in his throat. "Think carefully before you decide what you want this to be," he murmured, then straightened and stepped back as though nothing had happened.

Silence swelled in the space between them.

Nathan kept his eyes on the grain of the wood table before them, tracing the lines like a map, anything to avoid looking up and meeting Richard's eyes—because he knew that one glance could unravel every word he was about to say. The sound of the rain filled the room again, louder now, almost drowning him out.

Angela sat perfectly still in her chair. Her hands were clasped so tightly in her lap that her nails were digging into her skin. She didn't look at Nathan. She didn't look at Richard. Her gaze drifted past them, settling on the shadowed corner of the room. She swallowed hard, fighting the urge to speak up. If she said the wrong thing, would things get worse? The silence pressed against her, heavy and suffocating, but she didn't dare break it. Not yet.

She stared until the shapes blurred, she could almost imagine she was anywhere else—her office, a quiet beach, the old kitchen with the lemon curtains she'd loved. Anywhere but here. But as Richard's footsteps receded down the hall, Nathan still sat frozen beside her. Angela took a slow, trembling breath. She would have to do something. Not now…but soon.

The only movement was the slow rise and fall of her chest, as though she were afraid to breathe too loudly.

And Nathan felt it—in the quiet, in her stillness, she was already slipping away from him. At that moment, Nathan knew something was not right…and that whatever it was, it was only going to get worse. He didn't know how yet, but the line had been crossed. And in the quiet that followed, a decision began to form; he had to be ready for the next time.

It seemed as though—no matter how often Nathan came home from school, cleaned the bathroom, washed the dishes that Richard had left behind the night before, vacuumed the entire house, and mowed the lawn weekly—nothing ever seemed to be enough for Richard.

To keep from going home, Nathan lingered after school until the halls were empty, then wandered through leaf-littered sidewalks. Once, he ducked into a corner store for a soda, letting the cold can press against his cheek as the radio played an old track his mom used to hum while cooking. For those few minutes, the knot in his chest loosened. Then he stepped back outside, and the weight returned.

He sat on curbs, dragging out the time before he had to step back into the house. Home no longer meant safety—it meant bracing for the heaviness that settled in the air whenever Richard walked through the door. He spent more time at friends' houses or practicing with his band. Anything to escape the tension that clung to the walls of that house. Every word felt as if it might spark an argument, and silence was not much better. To stay out later, Nathan sometimes pretended to have extra rehearsals or study groups, finding peace in the noise of drums and guitars rather than listening to the sharp edge of Richard's voice.

Even when he came home, he would tiptoe to his room, headphones on, trying to drown out the stress with music. Being away became not just a preference, but a way of surviving the emotional weight that came with living under the same roof as Richard.

As the months passed, Nathan noticed changes in his mother that worried him. Once confident and assertive, Angela now seemed quieter, constantly second-guessing herself. Her once frequent and unrestrained laughter had grown rare, replaced by a distant, distracted look in her eyes. She moved through their home cautiously, as if afraid to take up too much space. Whenever Richard made a decision, Angela nodded quietly, offering no suggestions. Her eyes darted to Richard, searching for approval as if she no longer trusted her own judgment.

The small criticisms Richard had once reserved for Nathan gradually began creeping toward Angela, each remark chipping away at her identity with surgical precision. What started as mild disapproval soon became a steady stream of belittling comments masked as concern.

Over time, Angela began to question her own perceptions, feeling the weight of Richard's words as if they were truth. His constant criticisms made her doubt her instincts and her worth, slowly eroding her confidence. She started to believe that perhaps her kindness and patience were flaws, weaknesses that needed correction. The line between concern and control blurred, and her sense of self became increasingly fragile under Richard's relentless scrutiny, even as she tried to hold on to her sense of identity.

"You are too soft on him, Angela. He needs to learn how to take responsibility for his actions," Richard would say at dinner, his voice level, his tone calculated—not raised, but sharp enough to wound. There was a cold finality in his words that made disagreement impossible. It was not just criticism—it was correction, domination, a subtle reminder of who held power at the table.

Then his gaze would shift, fixing on Nathan with a penetrating glare. "I am not your father, Nathan. I am not Kacey; you will complete the tasks that are asked of you," he would say, his voice dipping into something darker. "In this house, you will follow my rules. And since you are sixteen now, when you think you can pay your own bills, you are free to go." He seemed to take pleasure in how the words landed, as if testing their boundaries and measuring how they prompted obedience. He justified every barb as necessary discipline and seemed to puff out his chest in vicious satisfaction. The words were not shouted but cut like a blade—sharp, deliberate, and meant to shame.

Angela's fork hovered above her plate, unmoving. Her knuckles whitened around the handle, but she didn't look up. It was the stillness of someone holding their breath, waiting for a blow to fall. The silence roared louder than any protest she might have given.

Nathan saw her shoulders slump lower each day, her laugh vanish like fog. It was as if he were watching color drain from a painting until only grayscale remained. The woman who once stood up for him, who once sang with him and laughed from her belly, now walked on eggshells in her own home.

When Richard cleared his throat, sharp as a warning shot, Angela's hand jerked, sending her spoon clinking against the side of the bowl. She froze, barely breathing.

It wasn't a single event that told Nathan something had changed—it was the accumulation. Fear revealed itself in patterns: a glance, a twitch, a silence too long to be natural. Angela's quiet transformation unfolded not in dramatic moments, but in ordinary ones. At the store, at the dinner table, even in the way she reached for a glass—each hesitation marked another step in her retreat from the woman she once was. One afternoon at the store, she held a carton of eggs, her fingers tapping against the box before she slipped it back on the shelf. "Maybe we should wait," she murmured, glancing toward the door as if Richard might walk in.

When Nathan spoke out of turn, Angela's shoulders tensed, and she lowered her gaze—her lips twitching into a tight, nervous smile as if silently begging the air not to shift. If Nathan spoke too quickly or too boldly, Angela's hand would tighten around her glass. "Let's *not*," she'd murmur, not looking at him, her voice shrinking with every word.

Over time, Richard's voice did not just fill the room—it became the room. His rules, his opinions, and his moods determined the climate of the house. Angela, once the center of their family, had become a shadow, shrinking in his presence.

Nathan felt his chest tighten. Each time his mother flinched at Richard's voice, a fire sparked behind his ribs—rage, helplessness, a desperate need to protect her. And yet he said nothing. Nathan's jaw clenched painfully as he swallowed his fear. He imagined standing tall, voice trembling but firm, forcing out the word "stop." But the image flickered, crumbling beneath the weight of doubt and the cold shadow in Richard's eyes.

If I speak, he'll turn on her. Or me. Or both. The thought settled like a stone in his gut, heavy enough to pin him to his chair. What if speaking up made things worse? What if Richard turned his anger on her again? The walls were closing in, but breaking them felt just as terrifying. He wanted to stand up and tell her she did not have to live like this, that love was not supposed to feel like fear.

But something stopped him every time. Not just fear—though that sat heavy in his gut like a stone—but the whisper of doubt that maybe he was the one overreacting. Maybe this was normal. That terrifying thought had roots, watered by every silence Angela held, every fake smile she offered Richard. So Nathan clenched his fists under the table. No, this wasn't normal. And yet, fear tangled with guilt and love, freezing him in place.

What if I make it worse? What if she breaks because I speak? The thoughts twisted inside him, a storm he couldn't quiet. His throat burned with unspoken truths, and still, the words never left his mouth. His silence was a cage—and, oddly, it felt safer than the unknown beyond it.

Richard's control was not just about rules or finances, but about erasure. He controlled the money, dictated whom Angela could talk to, and decided what she was allowed to wear, watch, or say.

There were no visible bruises, but the wounds ran just as deep—buried in silence, humiliation, and the slow dismantling of autonomy. The house, once filled with warmth and noise, had become a quiet battleground where Angela and Nathan moved carefully, always anticipating the next emotional land mine.

That evening, while Angela was in the kitchen, Nathan's gaze fell on a crumpled piece of paper tucked into Richard's coat pocket. Curious and instinctively wary, he quietly reached in and pulled it out. It was a hastily written letter, the ink smudged and uneven, revealing a raw, vulnerable side of Richard that Nathan had never seen before. It betrayed a confession of guilt, regret, and longing—Richard admitting to an affair, a betrayal that had been ongoing for months.

The letter was filled with apologies and promises to end the relationship, but also with lingering doubts and unresolved feelings that hinted at the chaos beneath the note's facade. Nathan's stomach clenched as he read it and felt the weight of a secret that threatened to shatter everything he thought he knew. Carefully, he folded the letter and slipped it back into Richard's pocket, knowing he had uncovered something far darker than he'd ever imagined.

Then, one morning, Nathan saw it.

Angela was reaching for a mug from the top shelf when the sleeve of her sweater slid up just enough to reveal the edge of a dark, spreading bruise across her wrist—angry and purple, a storm cloud trapped beneath her skin. It caught the light in a way that made it impossible to ignore, but she moved quickly, pulling the sleeve down without looking at him, without saying a word. Her face remained still, composed, practiced.

And in that moment, Nathan understood something even more terrifying than what he had feared: This was not new. She knew how to hide it. They never named it.

Angela's fingers clenched the fabric of her sleeve as she pulled it down with a speed that betrayed her calm. In her mind, she silently counted breaths—*one, two, three*—an echo of professional calm that now felt hollow. She avoided Nathan's gaze, terrified that the silent fear pooling in her own eyes would leap across to him.

Nathan turned away, swallowing hard. The bruise on her wrist was the conversation neither of them dared start.

Again, Nathan said nothing.

Not because he did not care—he cared so much it ached in his chest—but because the silence between them had grown thick and sacred, a protective layer they both feared breaking. Speaking the truth out loud might make it real. Might make it worse. So, instead, he watched her pour coffee with trembling hands and a hollow gaze, and he pretended not to see the way her fingers barely gripped the handle.

The bruise haunted him. Not just for what it was, but for what it meant—for how far things had already gone, for how deep Richard's reach had sunk into their lives. Nathan had long sensed the violence in Richard's words, in the way he isolated Angela, in the way he left her questioning herself after every conversation. But the bruise made it visible. Tangible. It was proof that love had long since left their home, replaced by control, fear, and survival.

Nathan never asked. Because in homes ruled by fear, survival often sounds like silence. In that silence, Nathan learned that violence was not always loud. Sometimes, it was the sound of a coffee mug being placed gently on the counter. Sometimes, it was the careful tug of a sleeve. Sometimes, it was watching the light in someone's eyes fade so gradually that you didn't notice it was gone…until, one day, you looked back and couldn't remember the last time it was there. And by then, it felt too late to get it back.

But even the quietest house eventually cracks beneath the pressure. The silence that protected them became the very thing that stifled them, and small tensions began to swell into sharp edges. Richard's anger had always been just beneath the surface, but now it simmered closer to the top, triggered by the smallest imperfection, the slightest defiance. Nathan could sense it coming, just as the air shifts before a storm. And then, one day, it happened.

Richard slammed the trash can's lid with a violence that echoed like a gunshot, his voice slicing through the living room like a whip. "Are you so lazy you can't handle one simple chore?" he thundered, each word heavy with disgust.

Angela flinched, her magazine sliding from her lap as if recoiling with her. The air crackled with tension. Nathan stood frozen, heart hammering in his chest, the weight of Richard's fury pinning him in place. It wasn't just anger—it was the kind of rage that made the walls close in, the room feel smaller, the silence unbearable.

Angela sat frozen, staring at her trembling hands. Her mind screamed to step in, to protect her son…but fear anchored her to the couch. If she moved, if she spoke, would he turn on her too? She clenched her fingers to keep them from trembling, willing herself to be invisible. *Don't make it worse,* she thought, the desperate plea repeating like a mantra. Another part of her brain—the clinician who could name trauma responses in others—shouted to break the cycle, but training and reality had never felt so far apart. Each second stretched, and she tasted the copper tang of fear at the back of her throat, but she still did nothing.

"I did not mean to forget," Nathan mumbled, but it did not matter. Richard was already walking away, muttering something about Nathan being a failure.

After that day, Nathan moved through the house like a ghost, silent and careful. He counted his steps. Held his breath. Memorized which floorboards creaked so he could avoid them, trying to stay out of Richard's way. But the more he tried to be invisible, the more Richard found reasons to belittle him. Every small mistake was an excuse for Richard to lash out.

It was a Friday evening when everything changed, when Nathan knew with a sickening certainty that his world was spiraling beyond his control. He had come home late from band practice. The night thick with tension, Richard stood in the center of the living room, a statue carved from threat. He did not speak at first. Just stared. Then he began pacing like a predator. As Nathan stepped inside, Richard's eyes flickered to him, cold and calculating, yet brimming with a dangerous, barely contained fury.

"You think you can just come and go as you please?" Richard's voice was low, controlled, but every word dripped with menace, a trap snapping shut.

"I told Mom I'd be late. We had practice," Nathan replied, voice trembling despite his efforts to sound steady. But the storm in Richard's eyes was enough to make his blood run cold. The air grew heavy, electric with impending violence, as if the room itself were holding its breath.

Before Nathan could react, Richard lunged, slamming him against the wall with such force that the air vanished from his lungs. His skull struck the wood with a sickening thud, stars bursting behind his eyes. For a moment, he couldn't move—stunned, breathless, the world tilting sideways.

"Don't you dare talk back to me, you little bastard. Do you hear me? Don't you dare talk back to me!" Richard snarled, his voice low and venomous. "You're under my roof. You follow my rules."

Angela burst into the room, breath ragged, one slipper dangling from her foot. Her face was paper-white, eyes wide with horror. "Richard, stop!" she cried, her voice cracking as she reached for him, fingers latching on to his arm as if it were the only thing anchoring her to reality.

He didn't flinch. His eyes blazed with something feral, and with a violent shrug, he threw her off. She stumbled back, nearly falling, as Richard retreated into the shadows—silent, coiled, and dangerous as a storm, waiting for the next strike.

Nathan stood shaking, fists balled at his sides. Every instinct screamed, *Run. Disappear. Fold into the wall and vanish.* But somehow—barely—he stayed upright. His heart pounded so loudly it drowned out Richard's voice. *Don't shake. Don't cry. Not now. Not in front of him.*

Then, with a cruel smirk, Richard's voice sliced through the silence like a whip. "That's what I thought, you little bitch."

Richard's words struck like blows before he even moved. For a long, brittle moment, the room held its breath. Nathan's pulse thundered in his ears, drowning out every other sound until all that existed was the space between them—predator and prey.

Richard's eyes glinted in the low light, daring him to speak, to flinch, to do anything that would justify the storm radiating off him. But Nathan didn't move. He couldn't.

His mother stood at the edge of the room, her hands trembling at her sides, mouth shut tight.

No one reached for him. No one stepped between them.

The silence was the worst part—thick, suffocating—broken only by the scrape of Richard's boot as he stepped back, not because he'd relented, but because he'd seemingly decided it wasn't worth the effort.

Nathan stood frozen long after Richard vanished into the hallway. Only when the darkness swallowed him entirely did Nathan realize he'd been holding his breath.

That night, Nathan knew everything had shifted. The ground beneath him had cracked open, and nothing—nothing—would be the same again. He felt the cold dread creeping into his bones. More terrifying than the bruises or the violence itself was the realization that the man he once feared as a bully had now crossed a line no one could ever uncross. And, worse still, his mother had stood there helpless, unable—or unwilling—to stop it.

Weeks passed, and Nathan could not shake the memory of that night. He began withdrawing even more, spending as little time at home as possible. He stopped talking to his mother, unsure of what to say. He did not blame her—he knew she was in a difficult position—but he could not understand why she was letting Richard treat them like this.

A few weeks after this incident, on a chilly afternoon, Nathan came home to find Richard and Angela arguing. He could hear the anger in Richard's voice, though his words were muffled through the walls. Nathan hesitated at the door, not sure if he should step in. But he pushed the door open when he heard his mother's voice break.

"You are always taking his side!" Richard shouted…

Nathan stood just outside the doorway, his entire body rigid. It wasn't just anger he felt—it was the memory of being eight years old, hiding in the closet while fists flew and words stung. This wasn't just about today. This was a rerun of every silent scream that had ever gone unheard. His face twisted in fury.

"You are coddling him, Angela! He is never going to grow up if you keep babying him."

"I-I am not babying him, Richard. He's our son," Angela replied, her voice trembling. Inside, she felt her pulse quicken as if she'd just stepped too close to a cliff's edge. She forced herself to hold his gaze, even though every instinct told her to drop her eyes and let the storm pass. Inside, a war raged, self-doubt pressing hard against her need to protect Nathan. Was she being too soft? Or had she just forgotten how to trust her own instincts?

"*Our* son?" Richard spat. "He is not mine, and he never will be. I am not Kacey, Angela. It's not my fault he's here. If it was up to me, he wouldn't even be here."

At that moment, Angela's voice shattered the tension with a piercing scream. "Richard, stop it!" she implored, voice trembling with fear and desperation.

Richard's eyes flashed with fury as he snapped back, "Get the fuck out of my house, Angela! I swear to God, if you don't walk out that door right fucking now, I will fucking tear you apart!"

Nathan's chest tightened, but it wasn't just anger—it was terror masked as fury. He was stepping into a storm with no armor, no guarantees, only the unbearable need to protect.

He couldn't bear to watch her like this—helpless, cornered.

He hesitated—just for a heartbeat—as fear gripped his chest like a vise. What if Richard turned on him? What if speaking up only made things worse? But the sight of Angela's shrinking form snapped something inside him. Heart pounding, he stepped forward anyway.

"Enough! Stop it! Just stop!" Nathan's voice broke the silence, raw and trembling with a mixture of fear and fury. The words escaped before he could second-guess, and as they echoed in the room, his chest tightened painfully—partly wishing he could swallow them whole, partly stunned by the courage that had found him at last. His hands shook, not just from anger, but from the raw fear of what Richard might do next. For a heartbeat, he almost wished he could pull them back, the silence after ringing louder than the shout itself. His knees felt weak, and his hands shook at his sides, but the words had burst out as if a dam had broken—uncontrollable and necessary. The words ripped out of him as though a wound had torn open—he wasn't sure if he was yelling at Richard now or echoing every time he wished someone had spoken up for him. "Stop talking to her like that!"

For a moment, everything seemed to freeze, and the room turned surreal. Nathan found himself standing there, a witness to a nightmare: his mother's husband looming over her, finger stabbing at her face.

Her hands came up halfway before she stopped herself, palms open, fingers trembling. She hated how small the gesture felt, how it looked like begging instead of defiance. The air was thick with violence, the kind that shakes your soul but leaves you paralyzed.

Richard spun around sharply, eyes narrowing into icy slits. For a heartbeat, Nathan feared Richard may hit him again, but instead, Richard sneered, a cruel, venomous smile curling his lips. "You are pathetic," Richard said softly, the words dripping with contempt. "Both of you."

In that instant, Nathan realized that the walls of their carefully constructed world were crumbling—he saw the darkness lurking just beneath the surface, a storm he could no longer ignore.

That night, Nathan lay awake in his room, arms stiff at his sides, as if his own body had become too small to contain what he now carried. The ceiling above him might as well have been a tombstone.

He knew he could not stay in this house any longer. Richard's words echoed in his mind, and he realized that this was not just about him anymore—it was about his mother. She was trapped, just as he was, and Nathan could not stand the thought of leaving her behind.

But what could he do? He was just a kid. Richard's grip on everything—on their lives, on her—seemed unbreakable. Nathan felt the crushing weight of helplessness settle over him, a ghost pressing against his lungs. Rage flickered inside him, sharp and wild, but it had nowhere to go. It just burned, a suffocating force that threatened to drown him. His fists clenched, trembling with rage and despair. He remembered his mother's face twisted with pain and fear, and a cold, fierce determination ignited within him.

He knew, deep down, that he couldn't live like this anymore. And though he didn't have a plan, he had something more dangerous—resolve. Tonight, he would begin looking for a way out.

But knowing what he had to do wasn't the same as having a way out. The silence in his room didn't comfort him—it pressed in from all sides, whispering that if he didn't act soon, there'd be no one left to save.

He could not allow his mother to suffer in silence, trapped in this nightmare. Nathan's chest rose and fell in shallow bursts, each breath jagged. His fists curled so tight his nails bit into his palms. The tears pressed hard behind his eyes, but letting them fall now would feel as if he were giving Richard something he didn't deserve.

And in that moment, amid the chaos, something inside him snapped as though a rope had been pulled too tight. It wasn't a decision. It was a scream he couldn't hold in anymore. One that would change everything. *I will find a way to get us both out.* That thought alone sent a ripple of fear through him. *What if I fail? What if Richard sees it coming?*

But under the fear was something else—a stubborn ember refusing to die. Even if it meant stepping into the fire with nothing but his bare hands. It didn't matter how far the fall was or how dark it got on the way down—he'd already stepped to the edge. He didn't have the plan yet, but he knew one thing for certain: He would fight with every ounce of strength he had. Because he refused to watch his mother drown in silence any longer. He would find a way. The decision didn't crash over him—it cracked through him, slow and sharp. Like ice breaking underfoot, each fracture made the ground less safe, but also made standing still impossible.

What if he was wrong? What if trying made things worse? Still, the weight of silence had become unbearable. He had to try because doing nothing meant letting the story end the way Richard wanted.

Nathan's decision to help his mother break free from Richard's control weighed heavily on him. What if no one believed him? What if this blew up everything? Still, silence was the more dangerous risk. He knew he could not take on Richard alone, but the idea of reaching out to someone for help made him uneasy. Richard was well-respected in the community and could charm anyone. Who would believe a sixteen-year-old over someone like Richard?

But he knew staying silent any longer wasn't an option. The weight pressing down on his chest was unbearable. If he stayed quiet, nothing would change; as a matter of fact, he knew it could get even worse. The next knock he made wouldn't be on his own front door. His mind raced with options, each more hopeless than the last. There was no map, no guarantee. Just the pull in his gut that told him staying would eat them alive and the cold truth that leaving could break them in other ways. Pretending wasn't survival anymore; it was surrender.

One afternoon, after school, Nathan walked aimlessly, the kind of walking that wasn't about getting anywhere but about outrunning something. The streetlights blinked on one by one, each hum echoing as though a heartbeat he couldn't steady. The world outside was still, almost peaceful—but inside a storm raged.

The silence of the streets only sharpened the chaos in his mind—screaming thoughts, jagged memories, and a thousand voices whispering doubt, fear, and the kind of shame that stuck to your skin like sweat.

His legs carried him forward, numb and mechanical, as if they belonged to someone else. Each step felt like treason—against the fear that kept him quiet, against the silent vow he'd made long ago to never speak Richard's name again. But the truth clawed at him from the inside, aching to be seen, to be heard even if it tore him apart in the telling.

Back in middle school, Mr. Harris had been the one steady thing in a world Nathan barely survived. Calm. Unshakably kind. The only adult who looked him in the eye without pity—or worse, indifference. The memory of his voice—low, steady, full of peace—still echoed when the noise got too loud.

Maybe he'll still listen.

Maybe he'll still believe.

Nathan stood frozen at the foot of the porch, his heart hammering so hard it felt as if his ribs might crack. The hanging wind chime clinked lazily in the breeze, each note tugging up a half-forgotten memory—his mom barefoot on the back deck, a pitcher of lemonade sweating in the sun, laughter rising into the warm air. The memory hurt.

The house in front of him was just wood and nails, but tonight it felt like a cliff's edge. One wrong move, and he'd go over.

Turn around. Pretend you never came.

No one will know.

You can go home. Pretend again.

His feet didn't move. His throat locked tight. He raised his hand…

Stopped halfway…

Lowered it…

Raised it again, shoving it forward before he could think himself out of it.

Three knocks…

Each one sharper than the last, like a pulse in wood.

Please. Help me. See me.

Stillness.

What if Mr. Harris opens the door and sees everything? The faint marks Nathan still hadn't named out loud. The tremor in his hands. The pieces of himself he'd worked so hard to keep hidden.

What if he opens the door and sees nothing at all?

Nathan's knuckles stung from the impact. He stared at the door, willing it to open, feeling the weight of silence press down.

You came this far. You can't back out now.

Please don't look away.

He knocked again, softer this time, as if gentleness might keep the truth from shattering everything.

When the door opened, Mr. Harris's expression shifted from surprise to alert concern. His gaze swept over Nathan—eyes, hands, posture—reading more than Nathan wanted him to. "Nathan," he said quietly, stepping aside, "come in."

The smell of old paper and wood polish wrapped around him like a blanket too thin for winter. He hesitated in the doorway, fear scraping at the inside of his ribs. Words were dangerous. Once spoken, they could never be pulled back.

But when he sank into the worn sofa, something inside him cracked.

It all came pouring out—not just what happened, but what it had done to him. The nights holding his breath in the hallway. The bruise on Angela's wrist she'd never explain. Richard's voice tightening the air until it was hard to breathe.

And his mother, frozen in the quiet, as if fear had become her skin.

Mr. Harris listened without interrupting, hands clasped, face still but not cold. Every so often, his jaw flexed—a flash of anger quickly buried. When Nathan stopped, drained, the silence that followed felt as if he were standing in the eye of a storm.

Mr. Harris leaned forward. "Nathan," he said evenly, "you're in a dangerous situation. I'm glad you trusted me, but you can't do this alone. Your mom needs help too, and we have to be smart about how we get it. Richard is dangerous. We can't tip our hand too soon."

Nathan nodded, a tear slipping free before he could catch it. Relief and terror twisted together in his chest. He didn't feel like a warrior. He felt as though he were a boy holding a blade that was too heavy—but holding it anyway.

Mr. Harris's voice stayed calm, but there was steel beneath it. "We have to be careful, Nathan. Richard thrives on control, and if we make the wrong move, it could make things worse—much worse. We need people who know exactly how to deal with this kind of man, and we need to act with precision."

He studied Nathan for a long moment, eyes narrowing slightly in thought. "I think the first step is finding a family therapist—someone your mom can trust enough to lower her defenses. Someone trained to help her see the full picture without feeling cornered."

Nathan's chest tightened. His mother was a therapist; she could read people like books, unravel trauma for others with a steady hand. But when it came to herself, she seemed blind to the storm around her. Would she believe another professional over her own instincts? Or would she fold herself back into denial?

A quieter thought crept in, unsettling and sharp: *Even healers can't carry everyone else's pain forever. They need someone to carry theirs too.*

Mr. Harris's voice cut through the weight in Nathan's mind, grounding him. "Sometimes," he said, his gaze holding Nathan's, "even the people closest to us need help seeing what's right in front of them."

After a long pause, Nathan nodded. Deep down, the decision had already been made—the lie they were living was too heavy to keep carrying. Pretending had become impossible.

In the weeks that followed, Mr. Harris took the lead, guiding Nathan through lists of practitioners who specialized in family dynamics and emotional abuse. Mr. Harris sent links, made calls, and kept circling one name: Dr. Molly Jennings—compassion without coddling, firm without force; years in the field, a reputation for balancing compassion with firmness, and the rare gift of making people feel seen without feeling pushed.

The name alone twisted Nathan's stomach. Convincing his mother to see her felt as if he were asking her to hand over a piece of herself she'd guarded for years. But Mr. Harris didn't flinch. "We'll find a way," he said with quiet certainty. "We have to."

Nathan knew it would require precision. Angela was proud, private—a fortress in heels. She had spent her career holding space for others, listening to the worst of their stories without ever showing the weight of it. To admit that she, too, was trapped in a story she couldn't fix—that would mean looking herself in the mirror without the armor.

So Nathan prepared to approach her as if walking on glass—slowly, carefully—hoping it wouldn't shatter before she heard him.

One quiet evening after dinner, Nathan found her alone in the living room. The lamp's yellow glow softened the shadows on her face but couldn't hide the fatigue etched into it. She was half turned toward the couch arm, a magazine open but unread in her lap. Richard was away on another business trip—one of those rare nights when the air in the house felt still instead of charged. Nathan knew moments like this didn't come twice.

He lingered at the doorway, hands shoved into his pockets, rehearsing the first words in his head and hating every version. Finally, he crossed the room and sat beside her, his weight sinking into the cushion with a small sigh.

"Mom," he said quietly, his voice brushing the edge of a whisper, "can I talk to you about something?"

She looked up. Her eyes softened instantly, but there was a faint wariness there too, as if she was bracing for a blow she couldn't see yet. "Of course, honey. What's on your mind?"

Nathan's chest tightened. His heartbeat thudded in his ears, drowning out the clock's tick. The words fought their way up before he could stop them. "I've been...worried about us. About how things have been since Richard moved in."

He felt his throat cinch tight. The words had scraped like gravel coming out, jagged and dangerous. *What if she doesn't believe me? What if she chooses him again?*

He forced the breath out. "Mom"—he met her eyes, his own burning—"he hurt me."

She froze. For a split second, her mind scattered—fear flaring first, then a hot rush of denial she couldn't hold on to. *He's lying,* a part of her tried to say, but the memory of that night—Richard's shove, Nathan's startled cry—rose up too fast to ignore. Her chest tightened as if her ribs were trying to hold in the truth.

"What are you talking about?" she asked too quickly.

He took a breath, ragged and shallow, every muscle trembling with the weight of the moment. "You saw it. That night. The way he shoved me. The way he always does—quietly, cruelly. Like it's nothing. Like *I'm* nothing."

Her lips parted, but no sound came.

"I know this is hard," he whispered, voice cracking, "but it's killing us. We can't keep living in this lie. We need help. Please…stop pretending this is okay."

Her face suddenly paled, eyes drifting away as if lost in some distant, unreachable place. Silence stretched painfully between them, thick with the weight of unspoken fears, shattered illusions, and years of secrets buried deep. Each second felt like an eternity, heavy and suffocating, pressing down on their shoulders, an anvil ready to crush them.

Finally, her voice broke the silence—barely more than a fragile whisper—trembling with helplessness, "I don't know what to do anymore, Nathan. I don't know how we got here. I…" Her voice faltered, tears threatening to spill over, trembling with the weight of her despair. "I just…don't know."

Nathan reached out instinctively, wrapping his trembling hand around hers and squeezing gently, a silent promise of support. "We don't have to do this alone, Mom," he said softly, voice thick with emotion. "I've found someone who can help us—a counselor. Her name is Dr. Jennings. I think we need to talk to her. Both of us."

Angela hesitated, her eyes shimmering with unshed tears, her breath catching as if fighting to hold back the flood. "Do you think that will help?" she asked, voice trembling.

"I do," Nathan said, voice steady despite the chaos inside. "We need someone who can see what's really happening—someone who can help us find our way out of this nightmare."

For the first time in what felt like forever, Angela nodded, her voice barely more than a whisper, trembling with fragile hope. "Okay," she whispered, "I'll go."

A week later, Angela and Nathan sat in the calming quiet of Dr. Jennings's office. The atmosphere was peaceful, designed to soothe, but Nathan's stomach was in knots, his heart pounding with a mixture of fear, hope, and uncertainty. Neither of them knew what awaited inside those walls, but both felt it—the fragile flicker of a chance at something better.

Angela sat tensely, her hands clenched tightly in her lap, trying desperately to stay strong for Nathan, even as the weight of everything threatened to break her apart. She reminded herself to breathe as she had told so many of her own clients: in through the nose, hold, out through the mouth. But the calm she had always taught felt unreachable. *What if I fall apart right here?* she wondered, the question pulsing in the quiet as loud as a scream she would never let escape.

When they were called into the office, a quiet tension hung in the air, thick and palpable. Dr. Jennings greeted them with a warmth that immediately softened the heaviness. She was a woman in her late forties, her eyes gentle yet piercing, radiating a reassuring calm that seemed to reach into their very bones.

Her office was a haven—dimly lit with a soft amber glow; plush, inviting armchairs; shelves lined with books and comforting knickknacks. It didn't feel like a sterile clinical space; it felt as if they'd stepped into a sanctuary, a safe harbor amid the storm.

"I'm glad you both came today," Dr. Jennings began, her voice smooth and soothing, like a gentle balm. Her words carried a quiet strength, reassuring them that they were not alone in this darkness. "I know this is difficult. I want you to know that I'm here to listen, to support you, and to help you find a way forward."

Nathan hesitated at first, the weight of silence pressing down on him. His mother, Angela, took a trembling breath, her eyes flickering with a mix of fear and hope. Angela slowly opened up, her voice trembling at first but gaining strength as she recounted their story—how the nightmare had begun, how Richard had once seemed so perfect, so charming, only to unravel into something darker. She described the subtle shift, the growing control, the creeping sense of entrapment. Her words spilled out, raw and unfiltered, as if releasing a long-held secret. Tears welled in her eyes, but she pressed on, desperate for someone to understand.

I have to say this out loud, or it will swallow me whole, she thought, surprised by the steadiness of her own voice as she peeled back layers of denial she had lived with for so long.

Dr. Jennings listened intently, her expression compassionate yet attentive, offering gentle nods and words of reassurance. She guided Angela with patience, helping her find her voice amid the storm of emotion.

Then it was Nathan's turn. His shoulders sagged as he spoke, his voice raw with emotion as he confessed the fear that had gnawed at him nightly, the anger that simmered beneath his skin, and the helplessness that had taken root over the past year. Nathan's voice cracked—finally, fully—as he exposed the raw terror that had eaten at him for years. The moments he felt powerless against Richard's growing menace. He didn't look at anyone. Couldn't. This was as naked as he'd ever been.

By the time they left that room, a fragile but undeniable sense of relief had washed over them. In the car, Nathan pointed out the crooked plastic flamingo in Dr. Jennings's neighbor's yard, and for the first time in weeks, Angela laughed without it sounding as if she were trying to.

The oppressive weight that had burdened their hearts felt marginally lighter, as if a crack had opened in the storm clouds. They knew the road ahead was long and uncertain— more storms would come—but for the first time in years, they'd decided they'd meet them side by side, not in silence. But in that moment, they were no longer alone. Dr. Jennings had shown them the first flicker of hope—a guiding light leading them toward reclaiming their lives from the shadows.

Chapter 2

RICHARD'S RETURN

*The realization was as terrifying
as it was freeing.*

When Richard finally came home from his latest business trip, the house felt as though it had caught its breath and was holding it tight—as if every surface was waiting, bracing for impact. The air was heavier, thick with years of silence screaming beneath the surface.

At that point, Nathan and Angela had been through three sessions with Dr. Jennings. The conversations were painful, the kind that opened old wounds, so fresh they bled again— yet in that bleeding, a strange clarity emerged. They began to see past Richard's mask, to the cracks beneath the polish, the fragility veiled by control. They recognized how he rewrote moments mid-sentence, how he twisted their words back against them until both mother and son doubted their own memories.

The realization was as terrifying as it was freeing. Angela's thumb scraped the edge of the kitchen table, a tiny, unconscious action she barely noticed. Normally, she would have folded her hands and lowered her gaze, retreating into herself. But, this time, she let her palms flatten on the cool wood. She leaned in, every muscle taut.

"I'm not going to apologize for the house not being spotless." Her voice trembled as if a leaf caught in a storm, but there was steel beneath the fragility. She didn't flinch. The familiar quiver crawled through her hands, but she made no effort to hide it. *Let him watch.* Her fingernails bit into her jeans beneath the table, anchoring her to the moment.

The ticking clock suddenly screamed between them, seconds stretching endlessly. She still couldn't meet Richard's eyes for long—not without her breath hitching—but her spine no longer crumbled under his gaze. Nathan saw the shift—the smallest of victories hidden in her posture. A flicker of hope kindled inside him, fierce and fragile. And yet, beneath it all, folded tight under his ribs, a cold fear coiled like a snake— defiance in this house always carried a price.

Richard's lips twisted into a smile too thin to warm the room. "Long trip," he said lightly, as though this were a casual greeting. "Would've been nice to come home to a little order."

Nathan's gut twisted at the facade. This was the mask Richard wore for the neighbors—the one polished to near perfection. To outsiders, he was the helpful man crouching by Mrs. Delaney's mailbox, tightening screws, smiling while she pressed a Styrofoam cup into his hand as thanks. Perfect. Polished. Untouchable. Inside, the true Richard was a storm coiled and dangerous.

That night, the mask cracked. Richard's eyes swept the living room with calculated disdain—the two empty coffee mugs, the forgotten blanket crumpled on the couch. "Why is this house such a mess?" His words fired like bullets, sharp and cold. He fixed his gaze on Angela, voice slicing through the silence, "What have you been doing all day?"

The words struck like stones and embedded in her chest. The old reflex to duck her head screamed to the surface, but the spark—barely a flicker—held her fast. "I have been working, Richard," she said, voice trembling but unyielding. She swallowed the urge to look away, held his gaze steady. "And I am not going to apologize for the house not being spotless."

Nathan's breath hitched—a taut wire ready to snap. He had watched his mother shrink so many times before, each time splintering something in his own soul. But, now, something inside him refused to break. "She said she's been working," he said, voice steadier than he knew he was capable of. "And you don't get to talk to her like that." For the first time in years, they stood together—mother and son—a fragile yet fierce front.

Richard's eyes narrowed, disbelief flickering before sharpening into something cold, almost predatory. His jaw clenched. Without a word, he spun on his heel, each step pressing venom into the floorboards. The slam of the door cracked the silence like a whip, dust lifting in the echo.

Nathan's shoulders released the tension he hadn't realized was there, and his breath rushed out in a shaky exhale. Angela's hands rested still on the table, eyes locked on the doorway. They had crossed a line—a boundary once invisible, now shattered.

Days slipped by with unnatural stillness. No footsteps echoed down the hall. No voice barked orders or took command. No Richard. But the silence was a different beast—empty, expectant, as if the house itself were waiting for the storm the quiet belied. And yet, life edged back in small, fragile moments. They laughed one evening over garlic bread so burnt even the dog turned away. They ate cereal for dinner and joked it was "gourmet night." Memories surfaced of brighter days before Richard's shadow had swallowed their home whole. Nathan caught his mother's genuine laughter one night—it startled him, a rare treasure to hold tight.

Later, Angela reached across the table. Her hand found his, the grip unexpectedly firm. "We're going to get through this," she whispered. "I'm stronger than I thought. And you…you're the reason I know I can."

Nathan looked away, unready to carry such weight. The stillness around them felt like a silent threat.

Men like Richard don't simply vanish. They wait. Patiently. Calculating. The text came in the dead of night, a cold light piercing the dark. "Miss me? I will see you soon."

Angela's breath hitched. Tears didn't fall; only a hollow ache carved deeper into her chest.

Nathan snatched the phone, pulse surging. It was no joke. No empty threat. It was a key turning in the lock of their fear. "We won't let him," Nathan vowed, voice low, fierce, but behind it lurked a shadow of doubt. He met Angela's eyes and saw the same raw fear etched deep, stubborn, a ghost refusing to fade.

Somewhere, in the dark corners of the world, Richard was plotting his return. And when he came back, the nightmare would truly begin.

Chapter 3

THE STAND

"We can't keep living like this," he whispered.

The courthouse loomed like a monument to judgment—stone and glass and silence pressing in from all sides. Angela sat rigidly on the wooden bench, her body humming with dread. She kept her eyes on a scuff mark in the floor, afraid that if she looked at the door, she'd see him—and worse, that he'd smile as though nothing happened.

Her eyes kept darting to the door, half expecting Richard to walk through it, wearing that mask of civility that had fooled everyone for so long.

Beside her, Nathan sat with his fists clenched in his lap, shoulders hunched as if he were bracing for an invisible blow. He hadn't spoken since they arrived. Every sentence he'd rehearsed in the shower that morning had scattered the second they walked through the courtroom doors, leaving him clutching silence as though it were the only safe thing left. Twice he opened his mouth, only to close it again, the words catching before they formed. But when he finally looked at her—eyes hollow, jaw tight—she understood without him saying a word: *We're really doing this.*

Months of fear coiled inside them like a second skin. Every slammed door, every muffled cry, every bruise hidden beneath a sleeve—it all sat with them in that courtroom, like ghosts in the pews.

Angela's stomach twisted as she scanned the room. So many strangers. *They'll hear everything. All of it. What if they don't believe us? What if he spins it...again?* She closed her eyes and gripped Nathan's hand harder. His was warm. Steady.

"We can't keep living like this," he whispered.

His voice was soft, but it struck her like a bell. She opened her eyes. He was scared—but standing. Just as she was. She nodded, swallowing her nausea. "No," she whispered back, "we can't."

A bailiff called their names. The courtroom rustled with the sound of shifting papers, distant heels, and shallow breaths. Somewhere behind them, a pen rolled off a desk and clattered to the floor, the small, ordinary noise oddly grounding in the midst of all that tension.

They stood when Kate Spencer entered, her presence commanding immediate attention. Dressed in a sleek navy-blue suit and heels that struck the tile with a purposeful rhythm, Kate carried a weathered leather case and the poise of a seasoned litigator.

"Follow me," she murmured, her tone even but urgent.

Kate Spencer had been practicing law for over two decades. She had seen her share of bruises, broken families, and desperate parents, but there was something about Nathan's hollow silence and Angela's haunted gaze that had carved this case into her heart.

The judge entered. A firm rap of the gavel called the courtroom to order. "Case number 34791. Parker versus Armstrong. Petition for a restraining order."

Kate rose immediately. "Your Honor," she said, projecting strength and restraint in equal measure, "this is a petition for a protective order. My clients, Angela and Nathan Parker, are seeking protection from Richard Armstrong, a man who has subjected them to sustained emotional abuse, threats, and coercive control. The trauma they've endured is real and recent. We have digital evidence, sworn testimony, and a timeline of escalating incidents."

Angela sat frozen while Nathan kept his eyes on the grain of the wood table before them.

The door creaked. A cold hush spread across the room.

Richard entered, crisp in a gray tailored suit, the faint scent of cologne trailing behind him. Only a week ago, a neighbor had seen him at the community center, handing out donated coats to families in need, laughing easily with the volunteers. He'd crouched to tie a child's loose shoelace, ruffled the boy's hair, and told the mother, "You've got a champ here." It was the kind of scene people remembered when they swore he couldn't be dangerous. He carried that same polished warmth into the room now, asking the bailiff about his kids and joking with someone in the gallery about the local baseball team, as if they were all old friends. The kind of superficial act that made strangers doubt anything truly dark could live beneath it.

He moved like a man with nothing to hide—confident, polished, nodding to someone in the gallery and mouthing "thank you" when a stranger held the door. It was the kind of civility that made people doubt the danger. Richard approached with a faint smile tugging at the corners of his mouth. To those unfamiliar with the case, he could have been any upstanding father, a businessman fighting to keep his family intact. He even nodded politely to the bailiff.

To anyone else, he might've looked like the wronged party—nodding politely to the clerk, thanking the bailiff for holding the door, even asking the court reporter if she needed a coffee.

Only Angela knew that smile was a weapon.

She saw through it. Her stomach coiled. Her breath shortened, and under the table, she dug her nails into her palms, willing herself not to react when Richard smiled as if the last year had been nothing but a misunderstanding. Her breath shortened.

"Your Honor," Richard began, his voice dripping with controlled indignation, "this is a misunderstanding. I've never harmed my family. My wife is confused, emotional."

Angela's jaw tightened so hard it ached, and she tightened her fists until her knuckles whitened. She kept her eyes on the judge, afraid that if she met Richard's gaze, she'd see the smugness she knew was there.

"We had our moments, but abuse? Never," Richard said and turned slightly toward the gallery, as if performing for invisible sympathizers.

Nathan's hand began to tremble. *He's fooling them again.*

Kate didn't flinch. "We've submitted screenshots of threatening text messages, voice recordings, medical notes, and statements from neighbors who've heard him screaming through the walls. What more evidence must a victim provide?"

The judge, stern and seasoned, leafed through the file. Her brow furrowed. "Mr. Armstrong, the court takes these accusations seriously."

Richard smirked. "Your Honor, I love my family. This whole thing? It's been blown out of proportion—"

"Mr. Armstrong," the judge interrupted, "do not belittle the proceedings. Do you have anything else to add in your defense?"

Richard paused, weighing his next move. Then, with forced resignation, he said, "Fine. Whatever you say."

The gavel came down hard. "Based on the presented evidence and testimony, I am granting the restraining order. Mr. Armstrong, you are to remain a minimum of one hundred yards away from Ms. Parker and her son. No contact—direct or indirect. Any violation will result in immediate legal action."

Richard's mask cracked. His nostrils flared. "This is a mistake," he hissed. "You'll regret this. Both of you."

The judge narrowed her eyes. "Mr. Armstrong, one more outburst and I will hold you in contempt of court."

Angela clutched her chest as if breathing finally felt possible.

Nathan's heart beat a chaotic rhythm against his ribs, but in that moment, he looked up. He saw the judge's eyes—steady. He saw Richard's retreating glare. And he saw, for the first time in a long while, the possibility of safety.

As the courtroom emptied, Angela and Nathan lingered, stunned.

Kate approached and said with a lowered voice, "He won't take this quietly. Call me the moment he steps out of line. Don't hesitate."

That night, they sat on the couch, side by side, surrounded by the silence of a home that finally belonged to them again.

Then Angela's phone buzzed.

Her blood turned to ice.

Richard.

She stared at the screen. Her hand trembled.

Nathan grabbed the phone. "Don't."

But she answered.

"You think this changes anything?" His voice was calm. Too calm. "You think a judge's little paper will protect you?"

Nathan snatched it from her ear. "Leave us alone, Richard. I swear, if you ever—"

Richard chuckled. It was low, guttural. "Oh, you'll see."

Nathan's hands shook as he dialed 9-1-1, the numbers blurring through the sting of adrenaline. For the first time in years, he wasn't just reacting—he was taking a step forward. It terrified him. It thrilled him. And it meant there was no going back.

The line had been drawn, and now they were waiting to see from which side Richard would try to cross it.

———————

That night, the house was too still.

Not peaceful…

Waiting.

Holding its breath.

Angela sat at the kitchen table, her hands wrapped tightly around a chipped mug of tea gone cold hours ago. She hadn't sipped it. Couldn't. Her fingers trembled slightly against the ceramic. The floorboards above creaked again, and her whole body jerked. Her eyes darted to the front door, her ears straining against the silence for something—anything—to betray the next rupture.

Upstairs, Nathan lay curled on top of his sheets, eyes half-lidded in a daze of exhaustion that never quite became sleep. He hadn't slept in days. Maybe weeks. His muscles always ached from staying ready. Every night, he'd listen… for breathing that wasn't his own. For doors easing open. For the past trying to come home.

And then—

CRASH.

Glass. Shattering. Not a cup. A window.

The sound knifed through the air.

Angela screamed.

Nathan shot up like a spring, his pulse a thunderclap in his ears.

The bat.

He dove for it from under the bed—wooden, nicked, a dull smear of dried dirt still on its barrel from last summer's game. It felt heavier now. Deadlier.

"Mom, go—into the pantry!" he shouted, already halfway down the stairs. "Lock the door and stay there!"

Angela stumbled out of the chair, barefoot and confused, the mug falling from her hands and shattering just as she made it to the pantry. Her hands fumbled with the lock as her breath came out in frantic gasps.

Nathan took the stairs two at a time, each footfall muted, careful, precise. He moved as if prey pretending to be predator. But the fear was a living thing slithering up his spine, coiling in his gut.

He reached the bottom and froze.

The living room was unrecognizable. Glass lay every-where—spilled diamonds under the moonlight. The window had been obliterated. Curtain rods dangled loose like snapped bones.

And in the middle of it all, silhouetted by the breach in the wall, stood *Richard*.

No weapon in his hands—

Because he doesn't need one.

His fists were clenched. His chest heaved. His shirt was ripped open, and his mouth was twisted into something both feral and eerily calm. He was smiling. As if he'd won something.

"Thought you could keep me out?" he rasped, voice low and shaking with rage. "This is *still my house*."

Nathan's feet refused to move at first. His hands tightened around the bat, but his palms were slick, and the thought hit him—*What if I swing and miss? What if it makes him angrier?* The questions rooted him for a beat too long before he forced his legs forward.

His hands tightened around the bat.

You have to do this. You're the only one here.

"You need to leave," Nathan said, voice hoarse. His grip on the bat tightened, but his knees felt unsteady, and a flash of doubt cut through him—if Richard didn't leave, then what? His throat tightened, but he forced himself not to step back.

Richard stepped forward, crunching glass under his boots. "I made this family. You think some fucking paper can stop me?"

"Get out." Nathan's voice cracked—but he didn't back down.

Richard laughed, wild and sharp. "Go ahead. Be a man. Let's see what your balls are made of."

Then…he charged.

Nathan swung too early. The bat whistled through empty air.

Then Richard was on him. A fist collided with Nathan's jaw. He spun, hit the ground hard, the breath exploding out of him. His vision blurred. He tasted blood.

Get up. Get up, or he'll kill her.

Nathan rolled just as Richard kicked where his ribs had been.

The bat—

He reached…got it…and swung from the ground, connecting with Richard's shin.

CRACK.

Richard howled, stumbled.

Nathan scrambled up, batting wildly. Not like a ballplayer. Someone trying to survive. The bat hit flesh. Then again. A forearm. A shoulder. Blood flew, dark and wet, splattering Nathan's face, his shirt. The sound—wood on bone—was sickening.

Richard tackled him into the wall. The drywall gave, caving under their weight. They wrestled, Nathan's hands finding Richard's face, shoving him back, gouging for space.

Angela screamed again from the pantry. "I'm calling the police! I'm calling— *Oh my God, Nathan!*"

But Nathan couldn't answer. Could barely think. His ears rang. His chest burned.

From the shattered window frame, Richard pulled a shard of glass—jagged, red with blood from his own hand—and *stabbed*.

The glass slashed across Nathan's shoulder, tearing fabric and skin. Hot blood poured down his chest.

But he didn't stop. He couldn't.

With one final roar, Nathan rammed Richard into the broken TV stand. The edge hit his spine. Richard dropped the glass.

Nathan raised the bat. "One more step," he whispered through gritted teeth, "and I swear to God—"

Flashing red lights sliced through the window.

Sirens.

Doors burst open.

"DROP IT! BACK AWAY NOW!" officers screamed.

Nathan staggered back, dazed, bleeding, eyes wide. His mind spun in jagged flashes—Richard's face, the blood on the floor, the sound of his mother screaming—and for a split second, he wondered if the sirens were real or just something his mind had conjured.

He dropped the bat. It hit the ground with a dull, wet *thud*.

Angela burst out of the pantry, face pale, tear-streaked. She collapsed beside Nathan, wrapping her arms around him. "Oh my baby, oh God, oh God…"

Richard screamed as officers pinned him down, his face twisted, foam at his mouth, blood staining the floor beneath his head. He fought them like an animal.

Still…he laughed.

A rasping, bloody laugh that didn't belong to any man.

And as Nathan sat against the wall, his shirt clinging wet to his chest, his shoulder burning, his heartbeat slowing just enough to hear the world again…he knew.

This isn't over.

It was a message.

A warning.

And whatever war Richard had started tonight…

Nathan would not run from it.

He would finish it. The thought burned hot, but beneath it, was a tremor he couldn't shake. Because finishing it meant facing Richard again, and part of him wasn't sure he'd survive that twice.

Chapter 4

PICKING UP THE PIECES

*I've helped people through this. Why can't
I do it for myself?*

The aftermath of the break-in left an almost sacred hush in the house—a silence so dense it pressed against Angela's and Nathan's hearts from every angle. Richard was behind bars now, finally charged with breaking and entering and violating the restraining order. The police had taken him away, their voices cutting through the chaos with calm directives, leaving behind confusion, relief, and a mess that was more than broken locks and shattered glass. But for Angela and Nathan, the damage Richard left behind wasn't something the police could catalog; it was a wound below the surface, invisible but profound.

The home they had once known—a place where Nathan's music played softly while Angela made tea, where they'd argued about socks and laughed about burnt garlic bread—sat in an uneasy quiet, each room holding its breath. Nathan moved through the wreckage with hesitant steps, gathering belongings scattered by Richard's search for something—control, perhaps, or just a fresh way to shatter their peace.

He tried to bring back life with the radio. A static-heavy polka station burst through the speakers, catching them both off guard. Angela let out a startled laugh, pressing a trembling hand to her chest. "Guess the universe doesn't need us sulking," she said, and for those brief seconds, the pain thinned as if sunlight were splintering the clouds. Nathan let the music play—awkward, bizarre—until the static won, and together they filled the silence with a kind of forced, determined normalcy.

But as the days stretched on, a more peaceful quiet reclaimed the house. It was fragile, always at risk of shattering under the weight of memory, the echo of Richard's anger still lingering in the corners. The walls seemed to sigh with the years of their family's history—both tenderness and trauma—while Angela sometimes caught herself staring into empty space, the ghostly shadow of Richard's presence flickering across her mind.

She would sit at the kitchen table, her fingers tracing the grain of the wood, and let the ache flood in. Her thoughts unspooled. *How was I so blind?* She replayed her trust like a bad movie, every scene sharpened by regret. She had wanted so badly to believe in the man Richard let the world see— thoughtful, neighborly, the one who remembered birthdays and helped fix leaky faucets for the couple down the street.

One morning, she watched Mrs. Delaney, across the hedge, handing out homemade muffins with a smile. Angela remembered the way Mrs. Delaney had thanked Richard. "Such a gentleman," she'd called him, her eyes kind and unknowing. The memory twisted inside Angela; she wanted to scream the truth, but could only swallow it down.

In therapy, seats shifted restlessly, and Angela wrapped her arms around herself, trying to shrink from the shame. "I feel like such a fool," she admitted, her voice breaking with grief and disbelief. "How could I have let him in? How could I have let him hurt us like that?"

Dr. Jennings offered a gentle nod, her patience a soft anchor. She watched Angela's shoulders curl inward, spotted the self-blame written in every clenched muscle. "Angela," she said softly, "abusers like Richard are masters of manipulation. They know how to charm and control. This wasn't your fault—none of it. You survived the only way you knew how, and you protected Nathan. That matters. It matters more than you realize."

Angela wanted to believe her. She fought against the tightness in her chest, the old voice whispering, *You should have seen this. You're no stranger to broken people. How could you miss it in your own home?* She nodded, blinking back tears, fingers curling around the edges of her knees as if holding herself together with the last threads of willpower.

Nathan's struggle ran parallel—a different melody, but no less discordant. He felt relief, true and deep, at the sight of police cars driving away with Richard inside. Yet guilt gnawed at him relentlessly. He remembered every glare, every word he'd spat in anger, every time he'd blamed Angela for not leaving sooner, not fighting harder. Rationally, he understood she was a victim too. His therapist had said it plainly, "Boys don't often recognize their mothers are running from battles they can't see." And still, at night, the resentment burned quietly under his ribs.

He'd never said it aloud—never would—but sometimes he wondered if, in another life, he could have done more. Could he have stopped Richard before the night everything broke apart? Could he have protected Angela better, been braver?

One night, as they sat side by side amid the remnants of Richard's fury—scarred furniture, patched window, bandaged hearts—Nathan let the thought slip into words. "Do you think it'll ever feel normal again?" he asked, voice a whisper, teacup in hand.

Angela paused, her eyes distant, lips curving before she answered, "Normal like when you were twelve and decided the toaster would be fine in your room?" she shot back. The memory tugged loose a burst of laughter—genuine, untethered.

Nathan grinned, for a moment feeling twelve again, the chaos not yet carved deep, the darkness not yet permanent. The moment glimmered, then faded. Silence folded around them, softer now, yet weighted—the kind born of grief and hope intertwined.

Angela set her cup down, fingers trailing along the rim. "I don't know," she admitted slowly. "Maybe normal changes. Maybe we learn to live with what happened, even if it's never the same."

Nathan nodded, swallowing despite the lump in his throat.

They kept going in small, patient steps: therapy every week—some sessions together, others in separate rooms where unspoken things could surface. Healing felt delicate, always at risk of shattering; it reminded Angela of glass— a wrong move and they'd be picking up shards again.

Nathan threw himself into college—chemistry lectures and late-night study groups, concert tickets with new friends who had no context for the scars he carried. He let the normal routines anchor him: unmade bed, laundry piles, heated debates about pizza toppings. In the spaces between classes and therapy, he felt a sliver of calm start to nest in his chest.

But nighttime eroded that peace. He'd lie awake listening to the wind twine around the house, the darkness pressing close, haunted by the memory of Richard's voice—threats hissing through the walls. Sometimes, he'd hear clattering outside and tense, every muscle waiting for the return of chaos.

Angela's journey was more solitary. She greeted mornings with a kind of muted determination, always awaiting a sound she prayed wouldn't come. Some days, the strength came easily—grocery shopping without checking every aisle for escape routes, walking to get coffee as if she belonged in her own skin. But there were mornings her hands trembled as she held her mug so tightly it left red marks.

Each small victory mattered: cooking dinner, laughing at Nathan's failed attempts to fold laundry, sitting in silence without flinching at every creak. Even washing dishes together, the rhythm familiar, gave her a rare sense of peace.

Some evenings, memory caught them off guard—a joke about burnt toast, or Angela teasing Nathan that "college kids need a laundry fairy," which he pretended to resent. These moments built up, thin slivers of sun breaking through the heavy clouds. Angela savored them; she knew how precious light was in the shadow of trauma.

Still, even on brighter days, old fears crept into the corners. Richard's presence remained, not in body but in habit and reflex. Angela caught herself listening for footsteps in the hall—phantoms from before.

Dr. Jennings was both a constant anchor and guide, her office a sanctuary filled with books and art. In one session, the air thrummed with a quiet tension. Angela braced herself for diagnosis, knowing how clinical language could feel like a verdict—especially for her, a therapist herself.

Dr. Jennings softened her tone and said gently, "You're showing symptoms of PTSD...some severe anxiety. With the trauma and manipulation you both experienced—those emotional wounds—this is how your mind tries to protect itself. It's not your fault."

Angela's mind raced—part professional, part survivor. She wanted to protest, to claim strength over suffering, but she simply nodded, jaw clenched against the truth. *I've helped people through this. Why can't I do it for myself?* The battle inside left her feeling exposed, like a frayed wire.

"So what does this mean?" she asked quietly, voice barely audible. "Are we broken forever?"

Nathan sat beside her, listening. He wanted to spill every fear, every protectiveness and reach for her hand—but worried touch might collapse her, make it worse. *She does her best. She keeps going, even when all is lost,* he thought fiercely, guilt and gratitude tangled in his chest.

Dr. Jennings leaned forward reassuringly. "It doesn't mean forever. Healing is messy—even on good days. You'll have setbacks. You'll have days when memories drag you down. But the act of facing it, of naming it—that's how you reclaim your story."

Angela met her gaze, tearful but steadier. "Do you think we'll ever really be okay?" The words hung heavily, more plea than question.

Dr. Jennings's answer was soft but sure. "Being okay may not mean going back to how things once were. It may mean finding peace going forward, living with the scars. What happened shapes you, but it doesn't define you."

Nathan felt a slow warmth stir—hope, fragile as new grass. "It's hard," he whispered, voice rough. "I keep thinking about everything, all the stuff we lost."

Angela nodded, her own voice thick with emotion as she turned to him. "It doesn't have to define us," she said, eyes searching his. "We survived, Nathan. We're still here. That means something. We're stronger than we think."

A hesitant smile flickered on Nathan's lips, tired but genuine. His heart let go of some weight, if only for a moment. "Yeah"—he breathed—"we are."

The session ended as sunlight faded, golden shadows stretching across carpets and bookshelves. Angela stared into the dusk, her mind balancing between pain and possibility. Nathan reached out, uncertain but resolute, letting his fingers brush hers. They felt the world shift infinitesimally—a first step forward, neither dramatic nor triumphant, but unmistakably real.

Weeks passed. Life moved with reluctant momentum. On walks through the autumn streets, Angela felt the chill—sometimes welcoming, sometimes menacing. The horizon glowed with streaks of orange, the air peppered with laughter from distant yards.

Nathan joined her on the porch, wrapping his hands around a mug of steaming tea, watching leaves tumble in the wind. The silence between mother and son filled with unsaid things—questions about the future, fear of repeating old mistakes. Finally, Nathan spoke—heart thundering. "Mom… do you think we'll ever feel safe again?"

The question wasn't about the locks or alarms; it was about the wounds inside, the vulnerability etched in both of them. Angela was quiet. She thought of the years lost, the pain endured, the small victories won. She thought of Mrs. Delaney waving and Richard smiling, his easy charm fooling so many…and knew there were battles invisible to outsiders, trust broken in places no one would see.

Angela's answer came softly, haltingly. "I don't know. But I know we're trying. We're building something new. Safety might look different now…but we'll keep reaching for it. Together."

Nathan nodded, a tentative hope kindling in his chest. The sky deepened to purple as twilight pressed close. For a long moment, they watched the horizon without words, listening to the chorus of distant voices, feeling the weight of what they'd carried and what they would become.

Home was not healed, not yet. But each step forward mattered: going to therapy, laughing, making dinner, forgiving themselves for days they stumbled. Angela found herself setting flowers in the window, listening for music instead of memory. Nathan studied long nights and chased dreams he hadn't dared consider before. In quiet companionship, scarred but determined, they began to stitch together a new life. It wasn't perfect—it was messy, vulnerable, but miraculous in its imperfection.

And as the wind whispered through the autumn night, Angela and Nathan understood that even in the longest darkness, the possibility of healing was real. Hope, battered but alive, could still bloom.

Chapter 5

A NEW BEGINNING

*There's always a way out—
even when the walls close in.*

They had come a long way since their world cracked open.

But distance wasn't measured in miles or seasons. It was measured in the ghosts they'd put to rest and the ones that still stirred in their sleep, restless and whispering.

The day Richard's sentencing was announced, the sky sagged low and gray, pressing on the courthouse like the weight of iron chains. The wind here cut sideways, slipping under scarves and inside coats, sharp enough to make Nathan's jaw ache. His hands dug deep into his pockets as if he could hide his pulse there, keep it from showing. Autumn leaves scraped along the wide stone steps, making brittle sounds that made him think of paper tearing.

He glanced at Angela. She stood next to him, spine rigid, eyes trained on the street beyond. Her collar was raised high against the wind, hair lifting in quick, erratic waves. One hand was buried in her coat pocket, but the other clamped her purse strap tight enough to whiten her knuckles.

Inside, not ten minutes ago, the gavel had fallen with a sound that seemed too small for such finality. Several years. Breaking and entering. Violation of a protective order. Words like cold bones, so stripped of heat they gave no indication of the living hell behind them. Not one syllable could capture the way their nights had carried a predator's footsteps, the vigilance that had lived in their muscles, ready to spring or cower.

Nathan had imagined this day differently—fiery, declarative. He thought justice might feel as if light were pouring back into their lives, allowing them to draw the first clean breath after being underwater too long. Instead, there was an uncomfortable stillness inside him, an anticlimax that felt almost unreal. The sentence was the full stop to a sentence that had begun years ago, but it didn't erase the paragraph.

―――――――

Beside him, Angela shifted and met his gaze. There was a flicker there—quick, sharp—fear before it melted into something else. She broke the silence.

"I think…we should move."

Her voice was so contained, riding just under the sound of the wind, but it landed inside him like a stone thrown into still water that now rippled outward.

"Move?" His reply was more reflex than question.

"This house"—she hesitated, dropping her eyes for half a breath before raising them again to hold his—"it holds too many memories. Every creak in the hallway…every shadow in the corner…they're his. I want the walls to stop whispering his voice. I want light in the windows that belongs to us alone."

Nathan's chest tightened. The thought of walking away from their house felt as if a limb were being cut off—it was the place that had hosted birthdays and arguments, his child-hood hiding spots, and the echoes of his father's laugh long before Richard. But then his mind flashed to Angela in the kitchen doorway, frozen mid-step because she'd heard a sound upstairs that wasn't there. He thought of how even laughter here felt different now—shorter, sharper, as if it wasn't sure it was allowed to stay.

He exhaled slowly. "Yeah," he said finally, feeling the word click into place, "you're right."

In the weeks after that, the house transformed into an obstacle course of boxes. Towers of cardboard leaned against bare walls like sentries. The air carried the sharp scent of packing tape, the dry dust of disturbed corners. Mornings bled into afternoons without much distinction, the hours marked only by the steady crumple of newspaper and the thud of sealed flaps.

Some boxes filled quickly—pans, plates, the comfortingly neutral background players of their lives. Others stopped her in her tracks. She would stand still, an object in her hand as if it had spoken to her. Nathan pretended to busy himself when those pauses came.

One afternoon, he pulled an ancient baseball cap from a box of old linens—bleached to a dull color by the sun, the brim bearing his childhood scrawl. A handful of folded notes with faded gel-pen writing followed, paper soft with age. And then, shoved behind a row of board games, he found the toaster.

Angela looked over, and her brows shot up before her mouth opened into a surprised laugh. It spilled out, unguarded, lighting her face in a way he hadn't seen in months. "I can't believe you didn't burn the house down with that thing."

Nathan grinned. "Had a system."

She shook her head, still smiling. For a moment, the room felt lighter—an air bubble trapped under deep water, rising toward the surface. The laugh faded, but not into the old silence. This quiet felt...gentler...as if it could be shared without danger.

Angela wrapped each item—fragile or not—with the same careful attention, her movements methodical but edged with thought. A blanket folded neatly could transport her to a winter morning when Richard's voice had turned sharp before the coffee had brewed. A coffee mug—perfect white ceramic—still seemed to hold the aftertaste of trips she had once mistaken for love.

Nathan learned not to fill those moments with sound. He knew now that she had to set some ghosts down by herself before she could pick up anything new.

Moving day came strangely stripped of drama, yet the air felt full, humming with unspoken things. The rooms, emptied, seemed at once bigger and smaller—bigger without the furniture, smaller without the life inside them. Dust floated in pale beams of midday light, drifting leisurely toward a floor swept clean of everything but memory.

Angela stood in the living room, her eyes tracing where frames had hung for years, where sunlight used to pool across the carpet. "It's strange," she murmured, almost to herself. "I thought leaving would feel heavier. But...I'm ready. More ready than I ever imagined."

Nathan studied her, noting the line of her jaw, the steadiness of her posture. Something in him clicked into alignment. "We're going to be okay, Mom."

Her eyes shone, catching the light. "Yes," she said softly, "we are."

The final click of the lock was barely audible, but it felt as if a door was closing on more than the building. The past still existed—but it no longer lived at this address.

The new house was smaller, but the stillness wrapped around them differently. Angela flinched at small sounds the first few days—pipes ticking, branches scraping glass—her body bracing on instinct, ears tuned to ghosts. When those noises faded without incident, her shoulders began to drop, her breath easing fraction by fraction. She found herself leaning into chairs instead of hovering at the edge of the seat, her hands curling around warm mugs in something close to comfort.

Nathan caught these changes as if he were someone spotting constellations—subtle shifts in position, the arc of her shoulders, how long her gaze lingered on a dusky sky without darting away in caution. Yet he still tracked every unfamiliar car that slowed near the curb, still noted the way some silences pressed too hard against his ribs. Old alarms didn't dissolve; they simply grew quieter, as if a radio's volume had been turned low.

One evening, months after that final lock had clicked, the sunset poured orange and pink over the street until it felt as though the sky were on fire just for them. The boards of the porch still held the day's warmth. Angela cupped tea in her hands, steam feathering her face.

Nathan sat beside her, listening to her inhale, slow and steady, like a measured claim on peace. "It's different here," he said, quietly enough that it might have been to himself. "I can breathe."

A small smile touched her lips. "I see that now too. There's always a way out—even when the walls close in. You showed me that."

Her words landed heavily. He wanted to tell her he hadn't always been brave, that there were moments he'd wanted to run but hadn't, moments he'd stayed silent when he should have fought. But he just sat with it, as if setting the truth down too roughly might break it.

In the months that followed, he thought often about what lay ahead: classes, friends who didn't know the old story, steps taken without glancing over his shoulder. He also knew Angela was still wrestling with forgiveness—not of Richard, but of herself.

He'd seen her, mid-trip to the store, stiffen at some half-remembered cologne scent in an aisle. Or her jaw tense when someone from the neighborhood mentioned Richard's name, surprised he was "doing time" because "he'd always been such a nice guy." Mrs. Delaney's banana bread had gone untouched after she'd said as much.

Richard's mask for the world had been nearly flawless. But now, in this place, it didn't matter. The act couldn't reach past their own walls.

Mornings for Nathan became a rhythm of running—pavement striking back under his shoes—lungs burning with the clean proof of air that was free to take, and sun cutting cleanly over rooftops were his daily reminders that they'd crossed the line into something new.

Angela began each day with a swift pull of the curtains, letting gold spill and spread unopposed across the floors.

They wandered shops with flowerpots out front and front doors that chimed when opened, meeting faces that smiled without the weight of knowing.

One night, Nathan played his guitar with the porch window open. The notes slipped into the cooling air, weaving between trees and lamplight. Angela listened from the kitchen doorway, eyes soft. When the last note faded, she spoke quietly but with certainty.

"I'm glad we're here. I feel like we can finally be ourselves."

Nathan almost said, *I still wait for the storm,* but didn't. Some truths could rest a while. He just nodded, letting her certainty stand.

It wasn't perfect. The shadows hadn't all left. But they had learned to live around them, instead of inside them.

Under a night sky thick with stars, Angela turned to him. "We aren't just surviving anymore."

Her voice carried the same tremor it had the day she'd said they should move—but now it shook from something else entirely.

Nathan felt the words burn into him, both fragile and fierce. "No," he said, "we aren't."

In the quiet after, they let their minds drift toward the future, not the fear. They talked about trips they might take, projects to try, people to invite into their lives without hesitation. They weren't simply hoping for better days. They had started to make them.

Chapter 6

THE POWER OF FORGIVENESS

Why didn't she see it sooner? Why didn't she protect us? Why didn't she protect me?

The weight of resentment sat in Nathan's chest like a stone; it grew heavier with each passing day. Three months had passed since Richard's arrest, three months since they'd moved to their new home, and still, Nathan found himself lying awake at night, his mind churning with questions that had no easy answers.

Why didn't she see it sooner? Why didn't she protect us? Why didn't she protect me?

The questions circled in his mind like vultures, picking at wounds that refused to heal. He'd catch glimpses of Angela making breakfast in their bright new kitchen, humming softly to herself as sunlight streamed through clean windows, and something ugly and familiar would surge—anger mixed with guilt, resentment tangled with love.

It wasn't fair. He knew it wasn't fair. But knowing something intellectually and feeling it in your bones were two different things entirely. *How do I forgive her when the anger still sits under my skin?* he wondered, ashamed of the thought even though he couldn't let it go.

One particular morning, Nathan sat at the kitchen table, staring at his untouched bowl of cereal as Angela bustled around, preparing for her day. She was getting ready to return to work—slowly, carefully, taking on just a few clients at first. Dr. Jennings had encouraged her to ease back into her practice, to reclaim the parts of herself that Richard had tried to strip away.

"I have a session with Mrs. Rodriguez this afternoon," Angela said, her voice carrying a note of cautious optimism. "She's dealing with some family issues, and I think I might actually be able to help her."

Nathan looked up and scrutinized his mother's face. There was something different about her now—a fragility that hadn't been there before, but also a strength that seemed to come from somewhere deeper than the surface confidence she'd once worn. Her hands trembled slightly as she poured coffee, and Nathan noticed the way she still flinched when doors slammed, the way she checked the locks twice before going to bed.

"That's good, Mom," he said, but his voice came out flat, hollow.

Angela paused, her coffee mug halfway to her lips. "Nathan? Are you okay?"

The question hung in the air between them, loaded with months of careful politeness, of walking on eggshells around each other's pain. Nathan felt something snap inside him— a rubber band that had been stretched too tight for too long.

"No," he said, the word coming out sharper than he'd intended. "No, I'm not okay."

Angela set down her mug, her face immediately shifting into the concerned, professional expression he'd seen her wear when talking to clients. But Nathan didn't want her therapist face. He wanted his mother—the woman who used to laugh at his terrible jokes and dance with him in the kitchen while they cooked dinner.

"What's wrong?" she asked, moving toward him.

But Nathan stood up abruptly, his chair scraping against the floor. "You want to know what's wrong?" The words tumbled out before he could stop them. "I'm angry, Mom. I'm so fucking angry, and I don't know what to do with it."

Angela flinched at his language, but Nathan was beyond caring about propriety. The floodgates had opened, and three months of suppressed rage came pouring out.

"I'm angry at Richard, obviously. I'm angry at the whole goddamn situation. But you know what really pisses me off?" He ran his hands through his hair, pacing now. "I'm angry at you."

The words hit the kitchen like a physical blow. Angela's face went pale, her hand reaching for the counter to steady herself.

"Nathan—"

"No, let me finish." His voice cracked with emotions warring between fury and heartbreak. "I know it's not fair. I know you were manipulated. I know you were a victim too. But, Mom, you're a therapist. You help people who are in abusive relationships. How could you not see what was happening to us? How could you not see what he was doing to *me*?"

Tears were streaming down his face now, and he wiped them away angrily. "I was sixteen years old. I was just a kid, and I felt like I had to protect you. Do you know how fucked up that is? I was more scared for you than I was for myself most of the time."

Angela's own tears had started, silent streams running down her cheeks. She opened her mouth to speak, but Nathan wasn't done.

"And the worst part? The absolute worst part is that I feel guilty for being angry with you. Because I love you, and I know you were suffering too, but I can't help feeling like you chose him over me. Every time you stayed quiet when he yelled at me, every time you made excuses for his behavior, every time you let him treat me like shit—it felt like you were choosing him."

The kitchen fell silent except for the sound of their breathing, both ragged and uneven. Angela looked as if she'd been slapped, her face crumpling under the weight of Nathan's words.

"I'm sorry," she whispered, her voice barely audible. "Nathan, I'm so, so sorry."

But Nathan shook his head. "I don't want apologies right now, Mom. I want to understand. I want to understand how someone as smart and strong as you could let that happen to us."

Angela closed her eyes, and when she opened them again, they were filled with a pain so deep it took Nathan's breath away.

"Because I wasn't strong," she said, her voice breaking. "Because I was scared and confused, and he made me doubt everything I thought I knew about myself. Because by the time I realized what was happening, I felt like I was in too deep to get out."

She moved to the kitchen island, gripping its edge like a lifeline. "You think I didn't see the signs? Nathan, I saw them. I saw every single one. But he had an explanation for everything. When I questioned his behavior, he made me feel like I was being paranoid, oversensitive. He convinced me that my professional training was making me overanalyze a normal relationship."

Her voice grew stronger as she continued, as if speaking the truth out loud was giving her power. "And when I did try to stand up to him, when I tried to protect you, he would withdraw his affection, threaten to leave, make me feel like I was destroying our family. He knew exactly which buttons to push, exactly how to make me feel like everything that went wrong was my fault."

Nathan felt some of his anger deflating, replaced by a crushing sadness. "But you're my mom," he said, his voice small. "You were supposed to protect me."

"I know," Angela said, her voice thick with tears. "I know, and I failed. I failed you in the most fundamental way a parent can fail their child. I was supposed to keep you safe, and instead, I brought danger into our home."

They stood there in the bright kitchen, surrounded by the trappings of their new life, but feeling the weight of their old wounds. The silence stretched between them, filled with years of unspoken pain.

Finally, Angela spoke again. "I don't expect you to forgive me, Nathan. I'm not sure I deserve it. But I need you to know that not protecting you is the biggest regret of my life. If I could go back and change things—"

"But you can't," Nathan interrupted, but his voice was gentler now. "We can't go back. We can only figure out how to move forward."

Angela nodded, wiping her eyes with shaking hands. "I've been seeing Dr. Jennings individually too," she said. "Trying to understand how I let it get so bad, trying to forgive myself. She says that healing isn't linear, that there will be setbacks."

Nathan felt a stab of surprise. He hadn't known his mother was in individual therapy. "What does she say? About the forgiveness thing?"

Angela managed a watery smile. "That forgiveness isn't about forgetting what happened or excusing it. It's about releasing the anger so it doesn't poison your future. But she also says it's a process, not a destination. Some days will be harder than others."

Nathan nodded slowly, feeling some of the tension leave his shoulders. They stood there for a moment, both of them raw and exposed, but somehow closer than they'd been in months.

"I don't know how to forgive you yet," Nathan said honestly. "And I don't know how to forgive myself either."

"Yourself?" Angela looked confused. "Nathan, what could you possibly need to forgive yourself for?"

Nathan laughed, but it came out sounding bitter. "For not being stronger. For not fighting back harder. For not protecting you better. For not somehow magically knowing how to fix everything."

Understanding dawned on Angela's face. "Oh, sweetheart. You were a child. You were doing the best you could in an impossible situation."

"So were you," Nathan said quietly, and they looked at each other with a new understanding.

The conversation marked a turning point for both of them, but it was far from the end of their journey. Over the following weeks, Nathan found himself cycling through different emotions—anger, sadness, guilt, and, sometimes, small glimpses of something that might eventually become forgiveness.

Some days were harder than others. There were moments when he'd catch himself watching Angela interact with others—laughing with their neighbors, chatting with the grocery store clerk—and feel a spike of resentment. *She can be normal with them,* he'd think. *Why couldn't she be strong for me?*

But there were also moments of grace. Such as the evening he came home from school to find Angela sitting at the kitchen table, crying over a thank-you letter from one of her clients—a woman who'd left an abusive marriage with Angela's help.

"She says I saved her life," Angela said, looking up at Nathan with wonder in her eyes. "How is that possible when I couldn't even save my own?"

Nathan sat down across from her, really looking at his mother for the first time in months. He saw the lines of pain around her eyes, the way she held herself more carefully now, as if she wasn't entirely sure of her own strength. But he also saw something else—a determination that hadn't been there before, a hard-won wisdom born from suffering.

"Maybe," Nathan said slowly, "it's because you know what it feels like to be trapped. Maybe that's what makes you so good at helping other people find their way out."

Angela's eyes filled with tears again, but these were different—tears of gratitude rather than grief. "Do you really think so?"

Nathan nodded, surprising himself with the sincerity in his voice. "Yeah, Mom, I do."

It was in Dr. Jennings's office, two weeks later, that Nathan finally began to understand what forgiveness really meant. He'd been talking about his anger, his guilt, the way he felt as if he were carrying around a backpack full of rocks that got heavier every day.

"Nathan," Dr. Jennings said gently, "what do you think forgiveness looks like?"

Nathan shrugged. "I don't know. Not being angry anymore? Pretending like none of it happened?"

Dr. Jennings shook her head. She could see the tension in his jaw and knew the word "forgiveness" might sound like betrayal. *Make it about freedom, not pardon,* she reminded herself. "Forgiveness isn't about pretending the hurt didn't happen or that it wasn't real. It's not about excusing someone's behavior or saying it was okay. And it's definitely not about forgetting." She leaned forward, her voice taking on the tone she used when she was about to say something important. "Forgiveness is about making a choice—a choice to stop carrying the weight of someone else's actions. It's about deciding that their mistakes don't get to define your future."

Nathan frowned. "But how do you just decide that? How do you just stop being angry?"

"You don't," Dr. Jennings said simply. "Not all at once.

Forgiveness is like physical therapy for your heart. You have to practice it, work at it, even when it hurts. And some days you'll take steps backward. That's okay too."

She paused, studying Nathan's face. "But here's what I want you to understand—forgiveness is something you do for yourself, not for the person who hurt you. You forgive because carrying around that anger is exhausting. You forgive because you deserve to be free from the chains of resentment."

Nathan felt something shift inside him, as if a door he hadn't even known was locked suddenly had swung open. "So it's not about saying what Richard did was okay, or that my mom didn't make mistakes?"

"Not at all," Dr. Jennings confirmed. "It's about saying that you refuse to let their choices steal your peace. It's about choosing to write the next chapter of your story instead of staying stuck on the painful pages."

That night, Nathan lay in bed thinking about what Dr. Jennings said. The anger was still there—he could feel it coiled in his chest like a sleeping snake. But for the first time, he could also imagine a future where it didn't control him.

The real breakthrough came a few days later, during one of his late-night conversations with Angela. They'd developed a habit of sitting on their back porch after dinner, watching the stars and talking about everything and nothing. It was during these quiet moments that their relationship was slowly rebuilding itself.

"I've been thinking about what forgiveness means," Nathan said, breaking the comfortable silence.

Angela turned to look at him, her face partially hidden in shadow. "What have you been thinking?"

Nathan took a deep breath. "I think I've been waiting for some big moment, you know? Like I'd wake up one day and suddenly not be angry anymore. But maybe it's not like that."

He paused, gathering his thoughts. "Maybe forgiveness is more like…choosing not to pick up the anger when it tries to grab hold of me. Maybe it's about remembering that you're my mom, and I love you, even when I'm hurt and pissed off."

Angela's breath caught. "Nathan—"

"I'm not saying I'm there yet," he continued quickly. "I'm still angry sometimes. I still have moments where I want to shake you and ask you how you could let it happen. But I don't want to carry this forever, Mom. I don't want Richard to win by turning us against each other."

Angela reached over and took his hand, her fingers cold but steady. "I don't want that either."

They sat in silence for a while, both lost in their own thoughts.

Finally, Nathan spoke again. "I need you to know that forgiving you doesn't mean I'm saying what happened was okay. It wasn't okay. And I need you to promise me that you'll never let anyone treat us like that again."

"I promise," Angela said, her voice firm. "I promise you, Nathan. I would die before I let someone hurt you like that again."

Nathan believed her. More than that, he could hear the steel in her voice that had been missing for so long. His mother was finding her strength again, building it back up from the ground.

"And I need to forgive myself too," Nathan said quietly. "For not being perfect, for not somehow fixing everything, for being angry with you."

"You have nothing to forgive yourself for," Angela said fiercely. "You were a child, Nathan. You survived. You kept us both alive by being brave enough to reach out for help. You have nothing to be ashamed of."

As they sat there under the vast canopy of stars, Nathan felt something loosening in his chest. The anger was still there, but it no longer felt as if it were suffocating him. It was just one emotion among many—sadness, love, hope, fear— all of them part of the complex tapestry of healing.

"I love you, Mom," he said, and for the first time in months, he meant it without reservation.

"I love you too, sweetheart," Angela whispered, tears streaming down her face. "More than you'll ever know."

Forgiveness, Nathan realized, wasn't a destination you arrived at. It was a path you chose to walk, step by difficult step, toward something better. And for the first time since their nightmare began, he felt ready to take that journey.

The road ahead was still long, and there would be setbacks, moments of anger and hurt that would test their resolve. But they would face them together, no longer as victim and enabler, but as two people who had survived hell and chosen love over bitterness.

In the weeks that followed, Nathan began to understand that forgiveness was indeed a daily choice. There were mornings when he woke up angry, afternoons when small things triggered memories of Richard's cruelty, evenings when he caught himself withdrawing from Angela out of old hurt.

But, each time, he made the choice to come back. To talk instead of sulk. To hug instead of hold grudges. To choose connection over isolation.

And slowly, gradually, the weight he'd been carrying began to lift. Not all at once, and not completely—he suspected it never would entirely disappear. But enough that he could breathe again. Enough that he could look toward the future with something approaching hope.

The power of forgiveness, Nathan learned, wasn't in the dramatic moment of absolution he'd imagined. It was in the quiet, daily decision to choose love over anger, healing over hurt, hope over despair.

And as he and Angela continued their journey together, he began to believe that maybe, just maybe, they really were going to be okay.

Chapter 7

BREAKING THE SILENCE

"I believe you now."

Nathan had been staring at the ceiling for hours when he heard his mother's soft footsteps in the hallway. It was 3:17 a.m. according to the digital clock beside his bed, but sleep felt impossible. The conversation about forgiveness earlier that day had stirred something deep inside him—something he'd buried so far down he'd almost convinced himself it wasn't real.

Almost.

He sat up in bed, his heart pounding with a familiar dread. There were things he'd never told anyone. Things that lived in the darkest corners of his memory, things that made him wake up in cold sweats, things that predated, by years, Richard's entrance into their lives.

The knock on his bedroom door was so soft he almost missed it.

"Nathan? I saw your light on. Are you okay?"

Angela's voice was gentle, concerned. She'd been checking on him more frequently since their conversation about forgiveness, as if she was afraid he might disappear if she didn't keep watching.

"Yeah, Mom. Come in."

In his doorway, Angela appeared wearing her old terry-cloth robe, her hair mussed from tossing and turning. "Can't sleep either?"

Nathan shook his head. "Too much thinking."

She moved toward his bed, but Nathan instinctively shifted away from her approach—a subtle flinch that stopped her in her tracks. It was barely noticeable, but Angela had spent years studying human behavior, reading the silent language of trauma in her clients.

"I'm just going to sit on the edge," she said softly, moving slowly and deliberately. "Is that okay?"

Nathan nodded, but she noticed how he pulled his knees up to his chest, making himself smaller. It was a defensive posture she'd seen countless times in her practice—the way survivors unconsciously protected themselves, even from people they trusted.

Angela sat carefully, leaving plenty of space between them. "Nathan, can I ask you something? And, please, feel free to say no if you're not comfortable."

"What is it?"

"When we were talking to Dr. Jennings about forgiveness, you mentioned feeling angry at yourself for not seeing the signs sooner. About Richard." Angela watched her son's face carefully. "But the way you said it... It felt like you were talking about more than just Richard."

Nathan's entire body tensed. His breathing became shallow, and Angela noticed the way his hands gripped his knees tighter. *Don't say it, don't say it,* he begged silently, a cold wash of shame making him nauseous.

"I was wondering," she continued gently, her therapist instincts fully engaged now, "if maybe your ability to recognize Richard's manipulation came from…prior experience. With someone else."

Nathan's face went pale in the dim light from the hallway. *How can I make her understand without reliving it?* he thought. His voice caught in his throat as he said, "Mom, I—"

"Because the things you knew to look for," Angela continued, her voice careful and measured, "the way you could see through his lies when I couldn't… That kind of awareness often comes from having survived something similar before."

Nathan's hands were shaking now. Angela could see the internal battle playing out on his face—the desperate need to finally tell someone warring with years of buried shame and fear.

"I keep thinking about your father," Angela said quietly, the words hanging heavily in the air. "About Kacey. About the way you used to flinch when he'd come home from work. The way you'd find excuses to stay in your room when he was around."

Nathan's breath hitched, and Angela knew she was right. Her professional training was screaming at her now, all the signs she'd been too close to see as a mother suddenly crystal clear through the lens of her expertise.

"The nightmares you used to have," she continued, her voice growing softer. "They started when you were four, right around the time things got really bad between your father and me. You'd wake up crying, but you could never tell me what the dreams were about."

Nathan was crying now, silent tears streaming down his face. His whole body was trembling with the weight of secrets he'd carried for far too long.

"And the way you reacted when Richard first moved in," Angela said, the pieces falling into place with horrifying clarity. "You weren't just being a difficult teenager, were you? You were seeing patterns. Recognizing behaviors."

Nathan nodded, unable to speak.

Angela felt her heart breaking as understanding dawned. "Nathan, did your father...did Kacey hurt you? Did he touch you in ways that were wrong?"

The question hung in the air like a live wire. Nathan felt his throat close up completely; all those buried memories came rushing back in a flood—images and sensations he'd spent years trying to forget, moments that had shaped every relationship he'd ever had.

"Nathan?" Angela's voice was barely a whisper now. "Sweetheart, you can tell me anything. Anything at all."

Nathan's vision blurred with tears he'd been holding back for so long they felt like poison in his system. His whole body began to tremble as the walls he'd built around the memories started to crumble.

"Mom, I"—his voice cracked completely—"I tried to tell you. God, I tried so hard to tell you."

Angela's face went pale. "What do you mean you tried?"

Nathan wiped his eyes with trembling hands, but the tears kept coming. The words fought their way out of him as if they had a life of their own, desperate to finally see the light after years of suffocating darkness.

"I was eight," he whispered, his voice so small Angela had to lean closer to hear him. "Maybe nine. You and Dad were fighting a lot, and you'd started working those late shifts at the clinic to avoid being home. When you guys separated, he had this girlfriend for a while, named Camille."

Angela's heart clenched. She remembered those months—the slow death of her marriage to Kacey, the way they'd barely been able to be in the same room without screaming at each other.

"Camille started coming into my room at night," Nathan continued, his voice becoming more mechanical, as if reciting it as a list of facts would make it hurt less. "At first, she said he just wanted to spend time with me, to make up for all the fighting. She would bring me snacks, read me stories. I thought...I thought she was being a good stepmom." Nathan's hands were shaking so badly now that he had to clench them into fists to make them stop.

Angela felt ice forming in her stomach. She wanted to stop him, to spare him from reliving this, but she knew he needed to tell it. Needed to finally let it out.

"She started touching me," Nathan said, his voice barely above a whisper. "She would shower with me and do weird things, and touch me."

Angela was crying silently, tears streaming down her face as she watched her son relive the worst moments of his childhood.

"It went on for months," Nathan continued, his voice completely flat now, emotionless. "Every night you worked late, and I would have to go to Dad's."

Angela wanted to reach for him, to hold him and tell him it was over, but she could see that Nathan was deep in the memory now, lost in that horrible time.

"But then, one night, I couldn't take it anymore. This was when Richard came into our life," Nathan continued, his voice growing stronger. "You came home from work, and I was sitting at the kitchen table doing homework, and you asked me why I seemed so sad all the time."

Nathan's face crumpled as he remembered. Memories didn't just return—they crashed. Each word he said felt like glass in his mouth. "I looked at you, and I said, 'Mom, Camille has been doing things to me. Bad things. When you're not here.'"

Angela felt the blood drain from her face. She had no memory of this conversation, which meant—

"But before I could explain what it meant," Nathan continued, "Richard came downstairs. He must have heard us talking." Nathan's voice changed, becoming cold and calculating as he mimicked Richard's tone, "'Angela, you know how kids Nathan's age can be. Their imaginations run wild. He's probably just acting out because of all the stress in the house.' Richard looked at me with a sharp stare and said, 'Nathan, you understand these are very serious accusations you're making, right?'"

Angela felt sick. This sounded exactly as if it were something Richard would say—always so rational, so quick to dismiss anything that threatened his carefully constructed image.

Angela gasped, the words hitting her like physical blows. She could almost hear Richard's voice saying those exact words, could picture the way he would have looked at

Nathan—not with anger, but with that cold, manipulative concern he'd perfected over the years.

"You looked between us," Nathan continued, his voice hollow now. "And I could see the confusion in your eyes. Richard seemed so calm, so reasonable. And I was just a scared little kid who couldn't even properly explain what was happening to me."

Angela felt as though she were drowning in guilt and horror. "What did I do? Nathan, what did I do?"

"You said maybe I was having nightmares…" His voice trembled. Even now, the sting of being dismissed hit deeper than any wound inflicted by Richard. Nathan whispered, "Maybe the fighting between you and Richard was giving me bad dreams, making me confused about what was real and what wasn't."

Angela's hands flew to her mouth as the full weight of her failure crashed down on her. She had failed to protect her child from the most fundamental betrayal imaginable, and then she had failed him again by not believing him when he'd tried to tell her.

"And Richard," Nathan continued, "he suggested maybe I should talk to someone professional. A child psychologist who could help me work through my 'confusion' about fantasy and reality. That's when I started seeing Dr. Eves, remember? Richard was adamant about me going to get professional help, and I went on a series of medications that made me even worse, even more anxious, and even more hypervigilant."

Angela felt sick. Even in trying to help, Richard had been manipulating the situation, making Nathan's truth look like delusion.

"I never tried to tell you again," Nathan said, his voice barely audible. "I figured if my own mother wouldn't believe me, nobody would. So I just…buried it. Pushed it down so deep I almost convinced myself it never happened."

Angela was sobbing now, her whole body shaking with the magnitude of what her son had endured—first the abuse itself, then the silencing, then years of carrying that burden alone. "Nathan," she whispered, "I am so sorry. I am so, so sorry. I failed you in every way a mother can fail her child."

Nathan looked at her with eyes full of pain but also something else—a desperate need for understanding. "That's why I could see through Richard so easily," he said. "Because I'd already learned what monsters sound like when they wear someone else's voice. Because I'd seen it all before. The manipulation, the gaslighting, the way predators twist reality to make their victims doubt themselves."

Angela understood now why Nathan had been so resistant to Richard from the beginning, why he'd seemed to have an almost-supernatural ability to see through Richard's charm. Her son had been protecting them both with hard-won knowledge that no child should ever have to possess.

"That's why I was so angry with you," Nathan continued. "Not just because you didn't protect me from Richard, but because…because you'd failed to protect me before. And I was angry at myself for not fighting harder, for not finding a way to make you believe me."

Her eyes welled up again. She reached for words and found none. In her silence, guilt gathered like dust on porcelain—fragile, but decades deep.

Angela reached out tentatively, and this time Nathan didn't pull away. She pulled him into her arms and held him as he cried—not just for the recent trauma with Richard, but for years of buried pain and unheard truths.

"I believe you now," she whispered into his hair. "I believe you, and I am so sorry it took me this long to see. You were just a baby, and you deserved so much better."

As they held each other in the predawn darkness, both of them broken but finally honest, Angela felt the true weight of what her son had survived. Not just one monster, but two. Not just recent trauma, but years of buried pain.

And through it all, Nathan had found a way to protect her from Richard when she couldn't protect herself. Her son—her broken, brave, incredible son—had used his own trauma to save them both.

The silence had finally been broken. The truth, no matter how devastating, was finally free. And for the first time in years, they both felt the possibility of real healing beginning to take root.

Chapter 8

WHEN THE DAM BREAKS

The silence in the house was deafening.

The silence in the house was deafening.

Angela sat on the floor in Nathan's bedroom, her back pressed against his dresser, watching her son sleep fitfully as dawn broke through his windows. She hadn't moved in hours. Every time she tried to leave, tried to process what he'd told her, her legs refused to work. The weight of seventeen years of motherhood—of protection, of failure, of love—pressed down on her chest like a stone. *How did I not see?* she asked herself over and over, the question looping through her mind until it was a chant. Every breath felt like penance, every heartbeat a reminder of the moment she had looked into her child's eyes and missed his terror.

Eight years old.

The words echoed in her mind like a death knell. Nathan was eight when Camille destroyed his innocence, and Angela had been too blind, too desperate, too broken by her failing marriage to see it. Worse—she'd silenced him when he tried to tell her the truth.

Nathan stirred, and Angela held her breath. When his eyes opened and found hers, something passed between them—a raw, electric understanding that everything had changed.

"You're still here," he whispered, his voice hoarse from crying.

"I'm not going anywhere," Angela said, but her voice cracked. "Nathan, I—"

"Don't." Nathan sat up abruptly, his face contorting with an emotion she couldn't name. "Don't you dare apologize to me right now. Between everything with Dad and then Camille, I was struggling but had no voice. When I finally felt like I had enough guts to say something to you, Richard swooped in, made my truth seem like it was an illusion, and you never followed up with me to even see if I was okay."

Angela flinched as if he'd slapped her. The apology she had rehearsed dissolved on her tongue. She wanted to fall to her knees, to beg for forgiveness, but a new resolve held her in place. *He doesn't need my guilt*, she realized with a jolt. *He needs my ears.* "But I need to—"

"No!" Nathan's voice exploded in the quiet room, months of suppressed rage finally finding its target. "You don't get to make this about your guilt! You don't get to cry and say you're sorry and make me comfort you!"

The force of his anger hit Angela like a physical blow. Nathan was standing now, his whole body shaking with fury that had been building for nearly a decade.

"Do you know what it was like?" Nathan's voice was raw, desperate. "Do you know what it was like to try to tell my mother—my own mother—that someone was hurting me, and have her look me in the eye and tell me I was confused? That I was making it up?"

Angela opened her mouth to speak, but Nathan wasn't finished.

"I was eight years old, and the person I trusted most in the world chose to believe a man she'd known for six months over her own son!" His voice broke on the last, tears streaming down his face. "I needed you to save me, but instead, you helped them bury me alive, Mom."

The words hung in the air like poison, and Angela felt something inside her shatter completely. Not just her heart—her entire sense of self as a mother, as a protector, as someone worthy of love. "You're right," she whispered, her voice barely audible. "You're absolutely right."

Nathan stared at her, his chest heaving, expecting her to defend herself, to make excuses. But Angela just sat there, taking the full weight of his fury, letting it burn through her.

"I failed you," she continued, her voice growing stronger even as tears streamed down her face. "I failed you in the most fundamental way a mother can fail her child. And there's no excuse for that. None."

Nathan's anger flickered, confusion replacing rage. He'd been prepared for her to argue, to explain, to minimize. Her complete acceptance of responsibility left him reeling.

"I can't take it back," Angela said, standing slowly, her movements careful and deliberate. "I can't go back and be the mother you needed when you were eight. But, Nathan, I'm here now. And I'm listening now. And I will spend the rest of my life making sure you never feel unheard again."

Something in her voice—a steel that hadn't been there before—made Nathan look at her with new eyes. This wasn't the broken woman who'd cowered before Richard. This was someone else entirely.

"How?" Nathan asked, his voice small. "How do we come back from this?"

Angela took a shaky breath. "I don't know. But we're going to find out."

The weeks that followed were a war zone.

Nathan would go hours feeling as if maybe they could heal; then something would trigger him—a news story about abuse, a song that reminded him of those dark nights with Camille, even just Angela reaching for him too quickly—and the rage would come flooding back.

One evening, as they sat in Dr. Jennings's office, Nathan exploded without warning.

"I keep thinking about all the times!" he said, his voice cracking. "All the times you hugged me after it happened, all the times you told me you loved me, all the times you acted like everything was normal when you knew— You had to know something was wrong!"

Angela tried to respond, but Nathan was on his feet now, pacing like a caged animal.

"I mean, I couldn't eat, couldn't sleep, couldn't think straight. And you would ask me what was wrong, and when I tried to tell you, you shut me down! You chose him over me!"

"Nathan," Dr. Jennings interjected gently, "what are you feeling right now?" She felt the heat of his anger and resisted the urge to defend Angela, focusing instead on grounding him. *Bring him back into his body*, she thought, anchoring her own breathing.

Nathan whirled on her, his eyes blazing. "What am I feeling? I'm feeling like I've been carrying this poison inside me for years! I'm feeling like the person who was supposed to protect me threw me to the wolves! I'm feeling like—" His voice broke completely, and he collapsed back into his chair, sobbing.

"Like you're drowning," Dr. Jennings finished softly.

Nathan nodded, unable to speak.

Angela watched her son fall apart, and something shifted inside her. The guilt was still there, would always be there, but something else rose alongside it—a fierce, protective love that should have appeared years earlier but was blazing to life now.

"Then let me throw you a lifeline," Angela said, her voice cutting through Nathan's sobs.

Nathan looked up at her through his tears, and Angela saw the eight-year-old boy he'd been—scared, hurt, desperately needing someone to believe him.

"I see you," Angela continued, her voice growing stronger. "I see what happened to you. I see how you survived it. I see how you tried to save us both from Richard because you recognized what I couldn't. And, Nathan…I see how extraordinary you are."

Something in Nathan's face began to shift.

"You want to know what I see when I look at you?" Angela leaned forward, her eyes intense. "I see someone who survived unimaginable trauma and still found ways to love, to care, to protect others. I see someone who could have let that abuse turn him cruel or bitter, but instead used it to develop an instinct for danger that literally saved our lives."

Nathan was listening now, really listening.

"I see someone who's been carrying wounds that weren't his to carry, shame that belonged to adults who failed him.

And I see someone who's ready to put that burden down and discover who he really is underneath all that pain."

But the real breakthrough came weeks later in the most unexpected way.

Nathan had been having a particularly dark day triggered by a nightmare that left him shaking and unable to eat.

Angela found him sitting on their back porch at sunset, staring at nothing.

"I don't know how to stop hating myself," he said without preamble when she sat beside him.

Angela was quiet for a long moment then asked, "What would you say to another kid who'd been through what you went through?"

Nathan looked at her, confusion flickering across his face. "What do you mean?"

"If an eight-year-old came to you today and told you that an adult had hurt them, that they'd tried to tell their parent but weren't believed, what would you say to that child?"

Nathan's throat constricted. "I'd tell them it wasn't their fault. I'd tell them they were brave for surviving. I'd tell them they deserved better."

"And would you mean it?"

"Of course, I'd mean it."

Angela turned to face him fully. "Then why can't you say those same words to yourself?"

The question hit Nathan like a physical blow. He opened his mouth to argue, to explain why it was different, but the words died in his throat. Because it wasn't different. He was holding himself to a standard he would never hold another victim to.

"Because," he finally whispered, "if I stop hating myself for it, then I have to face how much it actually hurt. And I don't know if I'm strong enough for that."

Angela reached out slowly, giving him time to pull away, and took his hand. "Nathan, you've already survived the worst part. You were eight years old, and you survived something that destroys grown adults. If that's not strength, I don't know what is."

Nathan felt something crack open inside his chest—not breaking, but opening. As if a door he'd kept locked for years had finally swung wide. "I want to feel normal again," he said, his voice breaking. "I want to be able to think about the future without it being colored by the past. I want to be able to trust people, to touch someone without flinching, to sleep through the night without nightmares."

"You will," Angela said with quiet conviction. "Maybe not completely, maybe not perfectly, but you will. Because you're not just a survivor, Nathan—you're a fighter. And you're not fighting alone anymore."

That night, for the first time in months, Nathan slept through the night without nightmares.

The healing wasn't linear. There were still setbacks, still days when the weight of the past felt unbearable. But something fundamental had shifted. Nathan was no longer drowning in his trauma—he was learning to swim through it.

Chapter 9

THE REVELATION

The nightmares still came,
but they were different now.

The nightmares still came, but they were different now.

Nathan would wake in the darkness, his heart pounding, but instead of the familiar terror that used to consume him, he felt something else—a burning need to understand. To make sense of what happened to him and, more importantly, to figure out how to help others who were drowning in the same darkness he'd barely escaped.

Three months after his revelation to Angela, Nathan found himself spending hours in the local library, pulling books on psychology, trauma recovery, and social work from the shelves. He'd start with one book and end up with a stack of five, reading voraciously about attachment theory, childhood development, and the long-term effects of abuse.

Angela would find him there most afternoons, hunched over a table in the back corner, taking notes in a composition notebook that was already half full. She never interrupted— just watched from a distance as her son devoured knowledge like a man dying of thirst.

It was during one of these library sessions that Nathan stumbled across a book that changed everything: *The Body*

Keeps the Score by Dr. Bessel van der Kolk. As he read about how trauma literally rewires the brain, how children adapt to survive impossible situations, how healing was not just possible but probable with the right support, Nathan felt something click into place.

This is it, he thought, his hands trembling as he turned the pages. *This is what I want to do.*

But wanting something and believing you deserved it were two different things.

That night at dinner, Nathan pushed his food around his plate, wrestling with a decision that felt too big for his eighteen-year-old shoulders.

"You're quiet tonight," Angela observed, refilling his water glass.

Nathan looked up at his mother—this woman who'd failed him spectacularly and then fought like hell to make it right. Who'd stood by him through the worst therapy sessions, who'd held him when the memories came flooding back, who'd never once suggested that maybe it was time to "move on."

"I've been thinking," Nathan said slowly.

"About?"

Nathan took a deep breath. The words felt huge in his mouth, as if they might change everything once he spoke them aloud. "About college."

Angela set down her fork, her full attention on him now. "College?"

"I know it sounds crazy," Nathan rushed on, the words tumbling out before he could lose his nerve. "I know my grades aren't perfect, and I know we don't have much money, and I know I'm probably not smart enough, but—"

"Nathan"—Angela's voice was firm but gentle—"slow down. What are you talking about?"

Nathan reached into his backpack and pulled out a crumpled college brochure he'd been carrying around for weeks. Riverside College's School of Social Work. "I want to study social work."

Angela stared at the brochure, then at her son, her expression unreadable. "Social work?"

"I want to help kids like me," Nathan said, his voice growing stronger with each word. "Kids who aren't being heard, who are being hurt, who need someone to believe them. I want to learn how to actually help, not just…survive."

Angela was quiet for so long that Nathan began to panic. *Maybe this is too much. Maybe she thinks I am damaged goods, that someone who's been a victim can never be a healer.*

"Nathan," Angela said finally, her voice thick with emotion, "you want to know what I think?"

Nathan nodded, bracing himself.

"I think you're the strongest person I know. And I think any kid who gets you as their social worker will be incredibly lucky."

Nathan felt tears spring to his eyes. "Really?"

"Really. But college is expensive, and competitive, and—"

"I know," Nathan interrupted. "I've been researching. Riverside has need-based financial aid, and Dr. Jennings said she'd write me a recommendation letter. And I've been volunteering at the crisis hotline downtown—Mrs. Patterson said she'd be a reference too."

Angela blinked. "You've been volunteering at the crisis hotline? When?"

Nathan flushed. "After our therapy sessions, sometimes. Just answering phones, but they trained me in basic crisis intervention. It's been…terrifying. And healing. Sometimes both at once." He searched for the right words. "Healing, I guess, to know that I can help someone else the way Dr. Jennings helped me."

Angela stared at her son with something approaching awe. While she'd been watching him heal, he'd been quietly building toward this moment. "How long have you been planning this?"

"Since I read that book about trauma," Nathan admitted. "Dr. van der Kolk talks about how survivors often become healers. How the people who've been through hell are sometimes the best at helping others find their way out."

Angela picked up the brochure, studying the photos of students in classrooms, practicum placements, graduation ceremonies. "Riverside College. That's three hours away."

Nathan's heart sank. "I know it's far, but their program is really good, and they have partnerships with agencies that work with at-risk youth, and—"

"Nathan"—Angela reached across the table and took his hand—"I'm not saying no. I'm just…processing. Three months ago, you could barely talk about what happened to you. Now you want to dedicate your life to helping other trauma survivors?"

Nathan was quiet for a moment, choosing his words carefully. "Remember what you told me in Dr. Jennings's office? About how I used my trauma to protect us from Richard?"

Angela nodded.

"I've been thinking about that a lot. About how surviving something horrible doesn't just have to be about surviving. It can be about…transformation. About taking the worst thing that ever happened to you and using it to make sure it doesn't happen to other people."

Angela felt her throat tighten. "That's a heavy burden to carry, sweetheart."

"It's not a burden," Nathan said, though part of him still trembled. But his voice…his voice…was steady, maybe for the first time since he was eight. "It's a purpose."

The application process was brutal in ways Nathan hadn't expected. Not because of the academic requirements—his grades were better than he'd thought, and his volunteer work had given him real experience to write about. The brutal part was the personal statement.

"Describe a significant challenge you've overcome and how it has shaped your goals."

Nathan stared at the blank document on his laptop screen for hours.

How do you write about childhood sexual abuse in 500 words? How do you explain that your stepfather's psychological manipulation actually taught you to recognize when someone was in danger? How do you turn your worst nightmare into college-application material?

He wrote seventeen drafts.

The first few were clinical, distant—the kind of essay written by someone trying to keep their trauma at arm's length. Dr. Jennings read them and gently suggested that admissions committees could spot emotional walls from a mile away.

"They're not asking you to relive every detail," she explained during one of their sessions. "They're asking you to show them who you are now because of what you've survived."

The breakthrough came during a particularly intense therapy session. Nathan finally stopped trying to minimize his experience and started honoring it.

"I was eight years old when I learned that not all adults can be trusted," he wrote in his final draft. "I was seventeen when I learned that some adults will use their power to silence children who try to speak their truth. But I was eighteen when I learned that surviving trauma doesn't make you broken—it makes you uniquely qualified to help others heal."

He wrote about his volunteer work at the crisis hotline, about the night a teenage girl called because her stepfather was touching her, and no one would believe her. About how Nathan was able to speak to her in a way that others couldn't because he understood the shame, the confusion, the desperate need to be heard.

"My goal is not to save everyone," he concluded. "My goal is to be the adult I needed when I was eight years old—someone who listens, who believes, who fights for children who can't fight for themselves."

Angela found him crying over his laptop at 2:00 a.m. the night he finished it.

"It's done," he said, looking up at her with red-rimmed eyes.

Angela read the essay over his shoulder, her own tears falling as she absorbed her son's words. This wasn't just a college application—it was a manifesto. A declaration that Nathan Parker was not going to let his trauma define him, but he was going to let it direct him toward something meaningful.

"Nathan," she whispered, "this is beautiful."

"It's honest," Nathan said simply. "For the first time in my life, I'm telling the complete truth about who I am and what I want. And I'm not ashamed of it."

The acceptance letter came on a Tuesday in March, thick and official-looking. Nathan's hands shook as he opened it, Angela standing beside him, holding her breath.

"Dear Mr. Parker," he read aloud, his voice trembling, "we are pleased to inform you that you have been accepted into Riverside College's Bachelor of Social Work program..."

Angela's scream of joy probably woke the neighbors.

Nathan just stood there, staring at the letter, feeling as if his entire life suddenly made sense. Yet behind the rush of adrenaline, a quieter voice echoed the doubt he still carried like a scar. *Do I really deserve this? What if I'm not the person they think I am?*

"I got in," he whispered. "I actually got in."

But even as they celebrated, even as Angela called Dr. Jennings and Mrs. Patterson and anyone else who would listen, Nathan felt a familiar flutter of anxiety in his chest.

What if I'm not ready? What if I get there and fall apart? What if I'm too damaged to actually help anyone?

The doubts came in waves over the following weeks. Some days, Nathan was exhilarated about his future, imagining himself in a classroom, learning about family systems and crisis intervention. Other days, he was paralyzed by the thought of leaving Angela, of being on his own for the first time since his world had imploded.

It was during one of these darker moments that Angela found him sitting on their back porch, staring at his acceptance letter with tears in his eyes.

"Second thoughts?" she asked gently, settling into the chair beside him. She knew that feeling well, not just as a mother but as a therapist. She watched the way he stared at the page and thought, *He's holding his breath, waiting for permission to be scared.*

Nathan nodded, not trusting his voice. If he opened his mouth, he feared the dam would break and reveal just how terrified he still was.

"Want to talk about it?"

"What if I can't handle it?" Nathan said finally. "What if I get triggered by a case and just...break down? What if I'm not strong enough to carry other people's pain when I can barely carry my own?"

Angela was quiet for a long moment, watching the sunset paint their backyard in shades of gold and amber. She mentally sifted through a dozen responses, discarding anything that sounded like a platitude. *Tell him the truth*, she decided. *Choose each word like it's a lifeline.* "You know what I think?"

Nathan looked at her.

"I think the fact that you're asking those questions proves you're exactly the kind of person who should be doing this work." Angela turned to face him fully. "Nathan, weak people don't survive what you survived. Weak people don't volunteer at crisis hotlines. Weak people don't dedicate their lives to helping others."

"But what if—"

"What if you help save a child's life because you understand their reality in a way that other people can't?" Angela interrupted. "What if your experience becomes the bridge that helps other survivors find their voices? What if your pain becomes someone else's healing?"

Is this what hope feels like? he wondered. He let the question settle, unfamiliar and exhilarating.

"You think I can really do this?" Nathan asked, his thumb worrying at the corner of a worn notebook. The question wasn't rhetorical—it was scary and real.

Angela smiled while reaching over to squeeze his hand. "Nathan, I think you were born to do this. Everything you've survived, everything you've learned, everything you've become—it's all been preparing you for this moment." She prayed he could hear the conviction beneath her reassurance. Prayed he knew she meant every single word.

As summer faded into fall, as acceptance turned into preparation, Nathan felt something he'd never experienced before when thinking of the future: excitement that wasn't overshadowed by his past.

The night before he left for college, Angela knocked softly on his door. She found him packing his books and notes with the same careful precision he once used to hide his secrets. "Are you nervous?" she asked gently.

Nathan paused, considering the question. "Yeah, but it's a good kind of nervous," he lied, trying to hide the swirl of dread in his gut. What if he failed? What if he didn't belong? "Like I'm finally ready to see what I can do when I stop hiding from who I am."

Angela hugged him tightly, and Nathan realized that her embrace no longer reminded him of helplessness. It reminded him of love—fierce, protective, and unconditionally supportive.

"I'm so proud of you," she whispered into his hair. "Not just for going to college, but for choosing to heal. For turning your pain into purpose."

Nathan pulled back to look at her, his eyes shining with emotion. "I couldn't have done it without you. Not the healing, not any of it."

"Yes, you could have," Angela said firmly. "You're stronger than you realize, Nathan. You always have been."

The next morning, Nathan loaded his car with everything he owned—which wasn't much. It felt like the beginning of everything. As he hugged Angela goodbye, he realized he wasn't running from his past anymore. He was carrying it with him, transformed from a burden into a compass pointing toward his future.

"Call me when you get there," Angela said, trying not to cry.

"I will," Nathan promised. "And, Mom? Thank you. For believing me. For fighting for me. For showing me that broken things can still be beautiful."

As Nathan drove away from the house, he thought of the home where he'd kept secrets for so many years. His hands tightly clutched the steering wheel. Each block felt as if he were crossing into unknown territory where he'd finally find the courage to speak his truth, where he'd learn that surviving was just the beginning. He felt something he'd never experienced before: genuine excitement about what came next.

He was driving toward a future where his voice mattered. But what if it failed him again? What if the trauma still stole his words when he needed them most? When his truth had power, when his ability to understand pain could help others find their way to healing.

The boy who'd been silenced was gone. In his place was a young man with a purpose, a calling, and the hard-won knowledge that the most beautiful thing about being broken is learning how to put yourself back together...and then helping others do the same.

For the first time in his life, Nathan Parker felt as if he might belong. Even if doubt still whispered, for once, it wasn't the loudest voice.

Chapter 10

NATHAN'S NEW LIFE

No more hiding. No more shame.

Riverside College buzzed with the electric energy of new beginnings. Nathan walked across the quad on his first day, backpack heavy with social work textbooks, feeling as if he was stepping into a completely different life. The boy who had spent years hiding was gone, replaced by someone who had a purpose, someone who belonged here. His introduction to social work class was held in a lecture hall that smelled of old wood and fresh possibilities. Nathan chose a seat in the middle—not too eager in the front, not hiding in the back.

As students filed in around him, chattering about their summers and their hopes for the semester, Nathan felt something he'd never experienced before: He was just another college freshman carrying the normal anxieties and excitement of starting over.

"Is this seat taken?"

Nathan looked up to find a girl standing beside him, auburn hair catching the morning light. "All yours," Nathan said, moving his backpack.

"Thanks. I'm Sophia Martinez," she said, settling into the seat beside him. "Social work major?"

"Yeah, you?"

"Same. Though I'm honestly not sure what I want to specialize in yet. You?"

Nathan hesitated. The truthful answer—trauma counseling—felt too heavy for a first conversation. *If I tell her the truth, will she see me as broken before she knows me?* he wondered, swallowing the urge to retreat. "Child and family services, maybe," he said. "Help kids who are going through tough situations…"

Sophia's face lit up. Her enthusiasm dazzled him; having a good childhood was a concept from a universe he had never visited.

"First day jitters, um…?"

"Nathan Parker. And yeah, definitely."

Sophia pulled out a notebook covered in colorful stickers—little sunflowers and peace signs that somehow made Nathan smile. "That's amazing. The world needs more people who actually give a damn about kids."

Something about her enthusiasm, her complete lack of cynicism made Nathan curious. Most people who went into social work had some kind of personal connection to social issues. But Sophia seemed genuinely optimistic, as if she was someone who'd grown up in a stable, loving home and simply wanted to make the world better.

Professor Williams entered the room then, a tall woman with silver hair and the kind of presence that immediately commanded attention. "Welcome to introduction to social work," she began. "Before we talk about theories and interventions, I want each of you to turn to someone you don't know and share why you're here. What brought you to this field."

Nathan's stomach clenched. He'd known this moment would come eventually, but he wasn't prepared for it on day one.

Sophia turned to him expectantly. "You want to go first?"

Nathan took a breath. "I guess... I know what it's like to feel unheard. To need an adult who would actually listen and believe you. I want to be that person for other kids."

Sophia nodded seriously. "That's beautiful, Nathan. Really."

"What about you?"

Sophia's smile was so bright it was almost blinding. "Honestly? I had this amazing childhood. Loving parents, stable home, all the advantages. And I've always felt like... Guilty isn't the right word, but responsible, maybe? Like I should use my privilege to help people who didn't get dealt the same hand."

Nathan stared at her. It was such a foreign concept—feeling guilty about having a good childhood instead of feeling ashamed about a bad one. "That's...really cool," he said, and meant it.

As the weeks passed, Nathan found himself gravitating toward Sophia in ways that surprised him. She was everything he wasn't—spontaneous where he was cautious, optimistic where he was realistic, trusting where he was guarded. She approached their social work classes with an enthusiasm that was infectious, raising her hand to ask questions that showed genuine curiosity rather than painful personal experience.

She invited him to study groups that turned into late-night conversations in the library. She suggested grabbing coffee after their human behavior class, which led to long walks around campus; she'd point out interesting architecture or comment on the changing leaves with the wonder of someone who found joy in small things.

Nathan kept waiting for the other shoe to drop. For Sophia to reveal some hidden darkness, some trauma that explained her interest in social work. But as October melted into November, as casual friendship deepened into something that felt dangerously close to romance, Sophia remained exactly what she appeared to be: a kind, stable, emotionally healthy young woman who simply wanted to help people. It terrified him.

"You're overthinking this," Angela said during one of their weekly phone calls. Nathan had finally mentioned Sophia—carefully, tentatively, as if afraid saying her name out loud might make her disappear.

"Am I?" Nathan was sitting on a bench outside his dorm, watching other students hurry past in their winter coats. Normal college students with normal problems and normal relationships.

"Nathan, honey, you're allowed to have good things happen to you. You're allowed to meet someone who doesn't have a tragic backstory."

But Nathan wasn't sure he knew how to be with someone who hadn't been broken. How do you explain hypervigilance to someone who'd never needed to be afraid? How do you share your triggers with someone who'd never had any?

The turning point came in December, during finals week. Nathan was stressed beyond belief—not just about exams, but about going home for winter break. Despite all his progress, the thought of returning to a place where he'd kept secrets for so many years still made his chest tight. He was having what Dr. Jennings would have called a "trauma response"—heart racing, palms sweating, that familiar feeling of being trapped even though he was sitting in his dorm room with the door wide open.

Nathan was sitting in the same place when Sophia knocked on the still-open door. "Nathan? Are you okay? You missed our study group." As he rose reluctantly and met her at the door, Sophia took one look at his face and pushed past him into the room. "What's wrong?" she asked, her usual brightness replaced by genuine concern.

Nathan wanted to lie, to make up some story about being tired or stressed about finals. But something about the way she was looking at him—not with pity or curiosity, but with simple human care—made him tell the truth. *She deserves honesty,* he thought, surprising himself. "I'm having a panic attack," he said quietly.

Sophia didn't ask why or demand explanations. She just sat beside him on his narrow dorm bed and started talking in a calm, steady voice about breathing techniques she'd learned.

When his breathing finally returned to normal, when the tightness in his chest began to ease, Nathan found himself telling her pieces of his story. With each sentence he waited for her to flinch, to look away in horror. But she didn't. And as she listened, a knot he'd carried for years loosened ever so slightly.

He didn't tell Sophia everything—not about Camille, not the details that still made him sick to remember—but enough. About Richard, about the emotional abuse, about learning not to trust his own perceptions of reality.

Sophia listened without judgment, without the horrified fascination that some people showed when confronted with trauma. When he finished, she was quiet for a long moment. "Thank you for telling me," she said finally. "I know that wasn't easy."

"Aren't you going to ask questions? Want to know more details?"

Sophia shook her head. "Nathan, your trauma isn't entertainment for me. You shared what you felt comfortable sharing, and that's enough."

It was such a perfect response that Nathan felt the air tighten inside him, as though the world itself were holding its breath. Maybe this could work. Maybe someone like Sophia could actually care about someone like him.

They started dating officially after winter break, though they'd been dancing around it for months. Sophia was patient with Nathan's boundaries, understanding when he flinched away from unexpected touch, never pushing for more intimacy than he was ready to give.

She celebrated when he aced his first-year classes, listened when he talked about his hopes of working with traumatized children, supported his decision to start seeing the campus counselor for additional therapy. For four months, it was everything Nathan had never dared to hope for. A normal relationship with a normal girl who happened to think he was worth loving despite his damage.

Which is why what happened in April caught him completely off guard. They'd been together long enough for

Sophia to talk about her family more casually. She'd mentioned her mom, Pamela, but always in passing—a single mother who'd worked hard to provide for Sophia, a mother who'd struggled financially but always made sure Sophia had what she needed.

"My mom wants to meet you," Sophia said one evening as they walked back from dinner in town. "She's driving up next weekend."

Nathan felt the familiar flutter of anxiety. Meeting parents was a big step, one that made their relationship feel more real and therefore more fragile. "Yeah, of course. I'd love to meet her."

But as the weekend approached, Nathan noticed changes in Sophia that he couldn't quite name. She seemed more tense, checking her phone obsessively, jumping at unexpected sounds. When he asked if she was okay, she brushed off his concerns with her usual bright smile, but something felt forced about it.

Pamela Martinez arrived Friday evening in a battered Honda that had seen better days. She was a small woman in her forties with Sophia's auburn hair and tired eyes that seemed to catalog everything around her. Nathan was immediately struck by how much older she looked than Angela, despite being roughly the same age.

"So you're the famous Nathan," Pamela said, looking him up and down in a way that made him uncomfortable. "Sophia talks about you constantly."

"Mom," Sophia said, and Nathan caught something in her voice—a warning, maybe?

Dinner was awkward in ways Nathan couldn't pinpoint. Pamela asked probing questions about his family, his finances, his plans after college. She made comments about Sophia's appearance—"You've gained weight, mija. College food, probably"—that made Sophia's shoulders tense. But it wasn't until they were walking back to Sophia's dorm that Nathan saw it happen.

Sophia was telling a story about one of their professors, gesturing enthusiastically as she talked. When she laughed and threw her hands up, Pamela's hand shot out automatically, grabbing Sophia's wrist hard enough to leave marks. "Don't be so dramatic," Pamela said sharply. "People are staring."

Nathan watched Sophia's entire demeanor change. The bright, animated girl he'd fallen for seemed to shrink into herself, her eyes going flat and careful. "Sorry, Mom," Sophia said quietly, rubbing her wrist. Nathan felt his stomach drop. He knew that look, that sudden shift from personality to survival mode. He'd lived it for years.

The rest of the weekend was a master class in psychological manipulation that Nathan recognized with sick familiarity. Pamela criticized everything about Sophia's life—her dorm room was messy; her clothes were too expensive for someone on financial aid; she was getting "too big for her britches" with all her college education. Every criticism was delivered with a smile, often followed by "I'm just looking out for you, baby" or "You know I only want what's best for you." Classic emotional abuse disguised as love.

Nathan watched Sophia transform throughout the weekend. The confident, optimistic young woman he knew disappeared, replaced by someone who walked on eggshells, who apologized for things that weren't her fault, who seemed to physically shrink whenever her mother spoke. When Pamela finally left Sunday evening, Sophia collapsed on her dorm bed and cried for an hour. "I'm sorry," she kept saying. "I'm so sorry you had to see that. I know she can be...difficult."

Nathan sat beside her carefully, his mind reeling. "Sophia, that wasn't difficult. That was abuse."

Sophia's head snapped up, her eyes wide with something that felt like panic. She could hear herself start to defend her mother and hated how automatic it was. *Don't make her the villain*, a reflex whispered, the same reflex that had kept her quiet for years. "No, she's not abusive. She's just...stressed. She works really hard, and raising me alone wasn't easy, and—"

"Sophia"—Nathan's voice was gentle but firm—"I know what abuse looks like. I've lived it."

"It's not the same," Sophia said quickly. "She never hit me or anything like that. She's just...critical. Demanding. But she loves me." Even as she said it, another voice inside her whispered, *Love doesn't leave bruises,* and the contradiction twisted like a knot in her stomach.

Nathan felt his heart break. He'd said almost those exact words about Richard to Dr. Jennings in the early days when he was still making excuses. "Love doesn't grab your wrist hard enough to leave bruises," Nathan said quietly. "Love doesn't make you apologize for laughing."

Sophia stared at him for a long moment, something shifting in her expression. Then she rolled up her sleeves. Nathan's breath caught. Sophia's arms were covered in small circular scars—cigarette burns, some old and faded, others more recent. Along her wrists and forearms were thin white lines that looked as if they'd been made by fingernails digging repeatedly into the skin. "She started when I was twelve," Sophia whispered. "When she started drinking more. She'd get angry about work, about money, about men who disappointed her. And I was...convenient."

Nathan felt rage bloom in his chest, hot and sharp. Not at Sophia, but *for* her. This beautiful, kind, optimistic girl had been systematically tortured by the person who was supposed to protect her.

"Why didn't you tell me?" he asked.

Sophia's laugh was bitter, nothing like her usual bright sound. "Because I knew you'd look at me differently. Because I knew you'd see me as damaged goods instead of just...Sophia."

"Is that what you think *I* am? Damaged goods?"

Sophia's eyes widened. "No, of course not. You're incredible, Nathan. You survived something horrible and turned it into a mission to help other people. You're like...a hero."

"And you're not?"

Sophia was quiet for a long moment. "I don't feel like one. I feel like a fraud. All that stuff I said about having a perfect childhood, about wanting to help people because I felt guilty for being privileged? It was all lies."

Nathan reached for her hand carefully, the way he would approach a wounded animal. "Why did you lie?"

"Because I wanted to be normal," Sophia said, her voice cracking, tears tracing silent rivers down her cheeks. "I just wanted to be normal. To be someone you could love without the shadow of ghosts trailing behind me. I wanted to be someone you could love without having to fix."

Nathan felt something shift in his chest, a recognition so deep it was almost painful. "Sophia, you think I don't have baggage? You think I'm not broken?"

"You're healing," Sophia said fiercely. "You're in therapy; you're pursuing your dreams; you're becoming who you're meant to be. I'm just...pretending to be someone I'm not."

"No," Nathan said firmly. "You're surviving. You're protecting yourself the only way you know how. Just like I did."

They talked until dawn, sharing stories they'd never told anyone. Sophia told him about learning to read her mother's moods, about becoming hypervigilant to any sign of anger or disappointment. About the cigarette burns that came when she "talked back," about the emotional manipulation that convinced her she deserved the treatment she received. Nathan told her about Camille, about Richard, about the ways trauma could make you doubt your own reality. About how healing wasn't linear, wasn't perfect, wasn't something you achieved once and then were done with.

As the sun rose over the campus, they made a pact. No more lies, no more pretending to be undamaged. They would figure out how to be broken people learning to love each other, scars and all.

But it was harder than either of them anticipated. Nathan's protective instincts went into overdrive. Every time Sophia's phone rang, he tensed, afraid it was Pamela. When Sophia had bad days—days when her mother's voice echoed in her head, telling her she was worthless, ungrateful, destined to fail—Nathan wanted to fix everything, to shield her from any additional pain.

Sophia, meanwhile, struggled with feeling like a burden. She'd spent years being told that her emotions were too much, that her needs were selfish. When Nathan tried to comfort her, part of her heard Pamela's voice. *You're being dramatic. Stop making everything about you.*

Their first real fight came in May during finals week. Sophia had been spiraling for days, convinced she was going to fail her classes and prove her mother right about college being a waste of time. Nathan had been hovering, trying to help in ways that felt suffocating to someone who'd learned to handle crisis alone.

"Just stop," Sophia snapped when Nathan brought her food she hadn't asked for. "I don't need you to take care of me."

"I'm not trying to take care of you," Nathan said, hurt. "I'm trying to support you."

"By hovering over me like I'm going to break? By treating me like I'm helpless?"

Nathan felt something cold settle in his stomach. "I don't think you're helpless."

"Then why are you acting like Richard?" The moment the words left her mouth, Sophia felt as if she had thrown a knife she could never retrieve. *Please, please don't let that be what he hears*, she thought, horror and regret colliding in her chest.

Nathan physically recoiled. His voice was barely a whisper when he asked, "Like Richard?" The name hit him like a slap. *Maybe I am becoming him.* Panic shot through Nathan's mind, drowning out everything else... *I'm acting like an abuser?* He felt his body moving before his mind could catch up, adrenaline hijacking his sense of proportion as he stood and paced, trying to outrun the thought.

Sophia immediately realized what she'd said, the devastating comparison she'd just made. "Nathan, I didn't mean—"

"I'm acting like an abuser?" Nathan's voice was getting louder, something desperate creeping into it. "I'm trying to help you, and you think I'm—"

"No, that's not what I meant," Sophia said frantically. "I just meant the controlling part, the wanting to fix everything—"

"The controlling part?" Nathan stood up abruptly, running his hands through his hair. "Jesus, Sophia, is that what you think of me?"

"Nathan, please, you're misunderstanding—"

"Am I?" Nathan's eyes were wild now, his worst fears crystallizing into horrible clarity. "Maybe you're right. Maybe I am just like him. Maybe that's what happens to people like me—we become the thing that hurt us."

"Nathan, stop—"

"My mother used to say Richard started out trying to help her too. Maybe this is how it begins. Maybe I'm just—"

"Nathan!" Sophia grabbed his hands, forcing him to look at her. "You are nothing like Richard. *Nothing* like him, do you hear me?"

But Nathan was spiraling now, caught in a fear he'd carried since the day he'd decided to go into social work. "What if I hurt you? What if I become controlling and manipulative and—"

"Nathan, look at me." Sophia's voice was firm, cutting through his panic. "You're having a trauma response. This isn't real. This is your brain trying to protect you by assuming the worst."

Nathan stared at her, his breathing ragged. "But what if—"

"What if I become like my mother?" Sophia said quietly.

"What if I start treating you the way she treated me? What if I get angry and say cruel things because that's what I learned love looks like?"

Nathan blinked, his spiral interrupted by the recognition that Sophia was voicing his own deepest fears back to him.

"Do you think I'm going to become abusive?" Sophia asked.

"No," Nathan said immediately, "of course not. You're nothing like her."

"Then why do you think you're going to become like them?"

Nathan sank back onto the bed, the fight going out of him. "Because I'm terrified," he whispered. "I'm terrified that everything good in my life is going to turn toxic because I don't know how to do this. I don't know how to love someone without being afraid I'm going to hurt them."

Sophia sat beside him, careful to leave space between them. "I'm terrified too," she admitted. "I'm terrified that I'm going to push you away because I don't know how to let someone love me without waiting for the other shoe to drop."

They sat in silence for a moment, both processing the weight of their shared fears. "So what do we do?" Nathan asked finally.

"I don't know," Sophia said honestly. "But maybe... maybe...we figure it out together? Maybe we learn how to be scared and still choose love?"

Nathan looked at her—this brave, broken, beautiful girl who'd been pretending to be whole for months to protect both of them. "I want to try," he said quietly. "But I need you to promise me something."

"What?"

"If I ever do anything that feels controlling or manipulative or wrong, you'll tell me. Even if it's hard. Even if you're afraid of hurting my feelings."

Sophia nodded. "Only if you promise me the same thing. If I ever lash out at you the way my mother did to me, if I ever make you feel small or wrong or inadequate, you'll call me on it."

"Deal."

They spent the summer working on their relationship with the same intensity they brought to their studies. Couples counseling sessions where they learned to recognize their triggers and communicate their needs. Individual therapy to work through their respective traumas. Long conversations about what healthy love actually looked like when both people were healing from abuse.

It wasn't easy. There were setbacks, fights that triggered both their defense mechanisms, days when they both wondered if they were too damaged to make this work. But there were also breakthroughs. Moments when Nathan could comfort Sophia without feeling as if he was being controlling. Times when Sophia could express anger or frustration without immediately apologizing or shutting down.

As their sophomore year began, they felt cautiously optimistic. They'd made it through the worst revelations, survived their first major fights, learned to see each other clearly without running away. A few days later, as October's golden hues deepened into the quiet, contemplative stillness of fall, Nathan found himself walking through the campus, lost in thought. The weight of everything—the past, the present, the uncertain future—pressed heavily on his chest. Then, his phone buzzed unexpectedly.

He glanced at the screen—a message from Sophia. "Can we talk? When you're free."

His stomach clenched. Not with fear, but with a peculiar mixture of anticipation and apprehension. He hesitated, fingers hovering over the keyboard. Then, with a shaky breath, he responded. "I'm free now. Want to meet in the park?"

He arrived at their usual spot beneath the towering ancient trees, their leaves whispering secrets in the cold wind. Sophia was already seated on the bench, her face calm but serious, her eyes holding a depth that made his heart ache. She looked up as he approached, and in that moment, Nathan saw the weight she'd been carrying.

She took a slow breath, her hands trembling slightly as she looked at him. "Nathan," she began softly, voice trembling with emotion, "there's something I need to tell you. Something I've been hiding for a long time. And I don't want to keep it inside anymore."

He sat beside her, feeling the tremor in her words. "You can tell me anything," he urged gently. "Whatever it is, I'm here."

Sophia looked down at her hands, then took a deep, trembling breath. "It's about the scars I hide," she whispered. "Not just the ones on my arms, but the ones inside. I've been afraid to show you. Afraid that if I do, you'll see me differently. That you'll see me as broken." Her voice broke slightly as she pulled her hands from the jacket's pockets. Slowly, she pushed up a sleeve, revealing the faintly scarred skin beneath. Then, with a trembling hand, she rolled up her sleeve further, exposing a series of small, fresh-looking cuts—crisscrossed, jagged, raw in places.

Nathan's breath hitched. His eyes widened in shock and heartbreak. "Sophia..." he whispered, voice thick with emotion. "Why didn't you tell me?"

Tears shimmered in her eyes as she looked away. Voice cracking, she replied, "Because I was ashamed. Because I thought if I showed you how much I've been hurting, you might see me as damaged...maybe even run away. I've spent so long feeling like I have to hide it all."

He reached out, gently taking her trembling hand in his. "You're the bravest person I know. You don't have to hide anymore. I love you—scars and all." Slowly, with a cautious gesture, he leaned in and pressed his lips softly to her wrist, where the scars marred the delicate skin.

Her breath hitched, but she didn't pull away. Instead, she looked at him with a fragile hope, waiting for his words.

"I love you," Nathan whispered fiercely, cupping her face with trembling hands. "And I love you exactly as you are. Your scars don't define you—they're just proof of everything you've survived, everything you've fought through. You're beautiful, stronger than I ever imagined. And I'll stand by you, no matter what."

In that moment, the quiet of the park seemed to hold its breath. The wind carried away the last of the leaves, whispering promises of renewal and resilience. Sophia's trembling fingers brushed his cheek, and her tears spilled over, blending with a soft, breathless smile. They sat there, wrapped in each other's arms, the fading sunlight casting a golden glow over their fragile, imperfect love.

For the first time, Nathan saw her not as someone who needed fixing, but as someone who was already enough. And Sophia, in turn, saw that she could be loved—completely, unconditionally—even in her brokenness. As they held each other close, a silent vow passed between them. No more hiding. No more shame. No matter what darkness lurked in their pasts or what storms threatened the future, they would face it together—stronger than their scars—bound by love that refused to fade. And in the quiet hush of the falling leaves, they knew their journey was only just beginning.

Chapter 11

BUILDING FOREVER

*Being scared is normal when
everything feels unsafe.*

Junior year arrived like a storm—relentless, demanding, and transformative. Nathan and Sophia had survived their freshman revelations, their sophomore growing pains, but nothing had prepared them for the intensity of advanced social work coursework combined with the weight of their deepening relationship.

At twenty-one, Nathan had grown into himself in ways that sometimes surprised him. His shoulders were broader now, his jaw more defined, but it was the confidence in his eyes that marked the most dramatic change. The boy who had once cowered in shadows now spoke up in seminars, challenged professors respectfully, and advocated fiercely for his future clients during practicum placements.

Sophia, also twenty-one, had blossomed in her own right. The girl who had hidden behind forced optimism now channeled her authentic experiences into powerful advocacy work. Her senior thesis on the intersection of childhood trauma and academic achievement had already caught the attention of several graduate programs.

But it was during their joint field placement at the city's children's crisis center that everything crystallized.

"Nathan, room three," their supervisor called out one particularly harrowing Tuesday morning. "Sophia, you're with me in intake."

Nathan knocked gently on the door before entering. Inside, a seven-year-old boy sat hunched in an oversized chair, his dark hair falling across eyes that held too much knowledge for someone so young. The intake notes were sparse but devastating: suspected abuse, removed from home the night before, refused to speak.

"Hi there," Nathan said softly, settling into the chair across from the boy. "I'm Nathan. You don't have to talk if you don't want to. Sometimes it helps just to have someone sit with you."

The boy—Marcus, according to his file—lifted his gaze for only a heartbeat, but it was enough. In those wary, too-old eyes, Nathan caught a flash of himself at eight years old. The same rigid, watchful posture; the muscles coiled as if ready to flinch; the flicker of instinct that measured every adult in the room for danger before allowing even the smallest thread of trust.

"I know you're scared," Nathan said, his voice pitched low, steady, like the hum of a lullaby without the melody. "I know you don't know who to trust right now. That's okay. Being scared is normal when everything feels unsafe."

Marcus's eyes widened ever so slightly—more reaction than most adults probably ever got. *Fear,* Nathan thought. *This kid has been taught it's a defect, a weakness. No one has told him it's allowed.*

So Nathan didn't press. For the better part of an hour, he just...stayed. No coaxing, no questions dressed as kindness, no fishing for details about whatever moments had shaped those brittle edges. He simply anchored himself there, letting the silence be a safe place instead of a pressure cooker.

When Marcus finally spoke, it came out as a whisper so soft Nathan had to lean in to catch it.

"Are you going to send me back?"

Something cinched tight in Nathan's chest, a rope pulled hard and fast. "No, buddy. You're safe now. We're going to make sure you stay safe."

Marcus hesitated, then lifted one small hand from where it had been wedged protectively under the opposite arm. His little finger extended slowly—tentatively, almost shyly. "Pinky promise?"

Nathan froze, the air between them charged. This wasn't just a child's game. It was a test. An invitation wrapped in vulnerability, asking in the only language Marcus could risk, *Will you break me too?*

He leaned closer, eyes locked on those impossibly ancient ones, and extended his own hand. Their pinkies hooked— gently at first, then a soft, deliberate squeeze, skin warm against skin. Nathan felt the slight tremor in the boy's grip, as if hope itself was a fragile thing that might startle and fly away.

"I promise," Nathan murmured. It wasn't the canned assurance of policy or protocol—this was marrow-deep, threaded with every vow he'd ever wished someone had made to him and kept.

And for a brief, breath-held moment, neither of them let go.

That evening, Nathan found Sophia in their usual spot in the library, but she wasn't studying. She was staring out the window, tears streaming silently down her face.

"Rough day?" he asked, sliding into the chair beside her.

Sophia nodded, unable to speak for a moment. "Twelve-year-old girl. Same age I was when…" She swallowed hard. "Her mother's boyfriend had been… And the mother chose him over her daughter."

Nathan reached for her hand. "What did you tell her?"

"That it wasn't her fault. That she deserved protection. That the adults who hurt her were wrong." Sophia's voice cracked. "But, Nathan, what if we can't fix this? What if we save some kids but lose others? What if it's not enough?"

Nathan was quiet for a long moment, thinking of Marcus, thinking of all the children they'd encountered during their placement. "Maybe saving one is enough," he said finally. "Maybe every child we help makes the whole system a little bit stronger."

"Is that what kept you going? The hope that your suffering might help someone else?"

Nathan considered this. "No," he said honestly, "what kept me going was people like my mom, like you, like Dr. Jennings. People who saw me as worth saving. Maybe that's what we become for these kids—proof that they're worth fighting for."

Senior year brought its own challenges. Graduate school applications, comprehensive exams, thesis defenses, and the looming question of what came next. Nathan had been accepted to several master's of social work programs, but his heart was set on the university's trauma-focused clinical track. Sophia had been offered a research assistant-ship studying resilience factors in abuse survivors.

They would both be staying in the same city, at the same university. It felt as if the universe were aligning itself with them.

But it was during spring break of senior year, on a quiet Sunday morning in April, that Nathan realized he couldn't imagine a future without Sophia in it—not just as his girlfriend, but as his partner in everything.

They were walking through the botanical gardens, a tradition they'd started during their sophomore year. Sophia was pointing out the early spring blooms, her face lit up with the genuine joy she'd learned to express freely.

Nathan stopped walking, his heart pounding with sudden certainty.

"Sophia."

She turned, still smiling, but the smile faded when she saw his expression. "Nathan? What's wrong?"

"Nothing's wrong," he said quickly. "Everything's right. That's the problem—no, that's not a problem. God, I'm terrible at this."

Sophia stepped closer, concern creasing her forehead. "Nathan, you're scaring me a little."

Nathan took a deep breath, reached into his pocket, and dropped to one knee right there on the garden path.

Sophia's hands flew to her mouth, her eyes wide with shock.

"Sophia Martinez," Nathan began, his voice shaking slightly, "two and a half years ago, I thought I knew what love was supposed to look like. I thought it was supposed to hurt, supposed to require you to disappear parts of yourself to make someone else happy. You taught me that love is supposed to make you more yourself, not less."

Tears were streaming down Sophia's face now, but she was smiling.

"You've seen me at my worst—panic attacks, trauma responses, the nights when I wake up fighting ghosts. And you've never once made me feel like too much or not enough. You've taught me that healing isn't something you do alone."

Nathan opened the small velvet box, revealing a simple but elegant ring—a vintage piece he'd found at an estate sale, delicate and unique, just like her.

"I don't know what the future holds, but I know I want to face it with you. I want to build a family with you—whether that's biological kids or adopted kids or the kids we help through our work. I want to grow old with you, fight for justice with you, heal with you."

His voice broke slightly on the next words. "Sophia, will you marry me?"

Sophia was crying so hard she could barely speak, but she managed to whisper, "Yes, oh my God, yes."

Nathan slipped the ring onto her finger with trembling hands, and when he stood up, Sophia threw her arms around him with such force they nearly tumbled into the flower bed.

"I love you," she whispered against his neck. "I love you so much it scares me sometimes."

"Good scared or bad scared?" Nathan asked, holding her close.

"Good scared." Sophia laughed through her tears. "The kind of scared that means something matters."

They graduated that May with honors, Nathan with a bachelor's in social work and a specialization in mental health counseling, Sophia with a degree in social work and a minor in psychology. Their families—Angela, Mr. Harris, even Sophia's grandaunt who had flown in from California— beamed with pride as they walked across the stage. Her mother's absence, etched by years of bitter estrangement, hung over the moment like a shadow that pressing on Sophia's chest, a silence too heavy for anyone to name.

The wedding planning was a careful balance of joy and practicality. Neither Nathan nor Sophia wanted a large affair, but they discovered they had more people who cared about them than they'd realized. Classmates, professors, fellow survivors from their support groups, colleagues from their field placements—their community had grown without them noticing.

They were married on a crisp October afternoon in the same botanical gardens where Nathan had proposed. Sophia wore her grandmother's pearl necklace and a dress she'd found at a vintage shop—simple, elegant, with long sleeves that covered her scars without hiding them. Nathan wore a suit that actually fit him properly, his hair recently cut, looking every inch the confident young man he'd become.

Angela clutched Sophia's arm as they stepped into the aisle, her tears falling freely, unbothered by the mascara streaking down her cheeks. Every step forward felt like a victory—against silence, against shame, against the years they'd both lost to pain. Sophia held her head high, but her fingers trembled slightly in Angela's grasp.

Mr. Harris performed the ceremony, having been ordained online for this very moment. As he stood before the couple, his eyes lingered on Nathan—not just the man he had become, but the shadow of the frightened boy who had once knocked on his door, drenched in rain and desperation. He remembered that night vividly: the rain clinging to the boy's skin like shame, his voice breaking under the weight of fear and longing for safety. And now, that same boy stood before him— tall, steady, loved. Pride swelled in Mr. Harris's chest, but so did the quiet ache of all the children he hadn't been able to save. *Let me do right by this one,* he thought, steadying his voice as he began.

When it came time for the vows, neither reached for paper. Their voices, raw and unshaken, rose from hearts unshaken by survival.

Sophia's voice quivered but held firm. "Nathan," she said, tears catching in her throat, "you taught me that love doesn't have to come with bruises or fear. You showed me what it means to be safe in someone's arms, to be seen and still held. You stood beside me when I couldn't even stand for myself. You've been my shelter, my truth, and my reminder that I am not too much to be loved."

Nathan's eyes glistened, his words heavy with the weight of everything he'd carried and everything he'd finally let go. "Sophia, you found me when I didn't know how to be found. You waited when I wasn't ready. You stayed when I doubted I was worth the staying. You've taught me that healing isn't always quiet—it's messy, loud, and brave. And you, Sophia, are the bravest thing that ever happened to me."

When Mr. Harris finally declared them husband and wife, the kiss that followed wasn't just a kiss. It was a benediction. Soft. Sacred. A seal on the promise that what had once been shattered could still become whole.

The reception took place in the old community center, a far cry from the lecture hall where they had first locked eyes in their introduction to social work class. Instead of chalk dust and shuffling notebooks, the air now carried laughter, clinking glasses, and the rustle of dresses against folding chairs. The space around them no longer echoed with beginnings but pulsed with celebration.

By night's end, with the tables empty and the music faded, Nathan and Sophia stood alone beneath the dim ceiling lights, still wrapped in wedding silk and hope. He pulled her close, and they swayed in silence, their rhythm slow and steady, like a heartbeat rediscovered.

Sophia laid her head on his chest. "We did it," she whispered.

Nathan smiled against her hair. "Did what?"

"We survived," she said breathily. "We survived long enough to find each other. We healed enough to let ourselves love. And, somehow, we built something beautiful out of everything that tried to break us."

Nathan pulled back to look at her, this woman who had become his wife, his partner, his future. "And now we get to keep building."

Three months later, they moved into their first home together—a modest three-bedroom ranch sitting on the edge of Cambridge. With a yard big enough for the garden Sophia wanted to plant, and the workshop Nathan dreamed of building. It wasn't much, but it was theirs.

The night they finished unpacking, they sat on their front porch, wedding rings catching the light from the streetlamp, and marveled at how far they'd traveled from the broken teenagers they'd once been.

At twenty-four, they were married homeowners, graduate students, and trauma survivors who had transformed their pain into purpose. They were no longer defined by what had been done to them, but by what they chose to do next.

"Ready for whatever comes next?" Nathan asked, taking Sophia's hand.

Sophia squeezed his fingers, her engagement ring clicking softly against her wedding band. "Ready."

As if on cue, a gentle knock came at their front door—the first visitors to their new home, though they had no idea who it could be at this hour.

Nathan and Sophia exchanged glances, curious and slightly apprehensive. Together, they walked to the door, ready to face whatever awaited them on the other side.

Chapter 12

BREAKING THE SILENCE

*The voice came like a cold draft
through a tight room.*

Three years later, Nathan and Sophia stood in the lobby of their newly opened practice, *Strength and Resilience Counseling Services*, watching the last strokes of paint dry on their new sign. Outside, the city moved in its usual rhythm—horns, footsteps, a bus sighing at the corner—but inside, the air carried the warm smell of fresh coffee and the lemon polish Sophia insisted on using for the reception desk.

At twenty-seven, they'd done something neither of them had dared dream back in grad school—built a thriving trauma practice with a focus on an underserved and often-doubted population: male survivors of domestic violence.

Nathan stepped back from the entrance and took in the space as if he were a gardener admiring a first harvest. The waiting room breathed calm—soft lighting, deep armchairs in earth tones, a bowl of smooth river stones on the side table, and artwork Sophia picked for quiet optimism rather than platitudes. One canvas showed a single wind-bent tree rooted in a bluff. "Hope without the cheesy rainbows," she'd said when it arrived, grinning.

"Remember when we thought we'd never get past five clients?" Sophia asked now, adjusting by a millimeter the frame around their practice license.

Nathan slid his arms around her waist from behind and let his chin rest on her shoulder. "Now we have a waiting list. And three other therapists who actually argue about who gets to run group."

She laughed softly. "You still talk like it happened by accident."

"Some of the best things do," he said, kissing her temple.

Their specialty had taken shape almost by gravity. During supervised hours, Nathan kept encountering a pattern—men who, once they felt truly safe, disclosed abuse. Sometimes it was in words honed like blades—humiliation, isolation, financial control. Sometimes it was with bruises, objects thrown, locks on doors. Sometimes it was in descriptions of sexual violence wrapped in the language of "jokes" or "punishment." Almost all of them carried shame like a second spine.

"Men aren't supposed to be victims," their first male client, Marcus—a thirty-four-year-old construction worker—had said at intake, voice steady but hands trembling. "My wife throws things at me, tells me I'm worthless, controls every dollar I make. If I tell anybody, they'll either laugh or ask what I did to deserve it."

Nathan had watched Marcus stare at his boots, bracing for mockery that didn't come. That session peeled back a hidden layer: Nathan's own history—surviving Richard's abuse—wasn't an isolated disaster; it was part of a broader, undercounted epidemic.

He started reading at night, highlighter in hand. One in four men experience domestic violence across a lifetime. Most never report it. Fewer get real help.

"We have to build something for them," he'd told Sophia over late-night noodles at their scarred kitchen table. "A place where they don't have to defend their right to feel pain before they can get help."

She'd nodded, eyes bright. Her research focused on how gender stereotypes shape trauma recovery. "A place where 'strong' and 'survivor' aren't opposites," she said.

Together, with steady steps, they built a program: safety planning, body-based grounding, skills for boundaries and de-escalation, and a group space that, without reservation, treated men's stories as real.

Their approach was simple but different: give men room to tell the truth without being told to "man up," validate without hedging, and build healing that didn't require discarding identity. They added couples work for survivors and their partners, family sessions where kids could relearn trust, and groups tailored to specific experiences—childhood abuse, veterans' issues, men in same-sex relationships.

Word of mouth did the rest. Marcus referred his brother-in-law. The brother-in-law told a coworker. The coworker brought a neighbor who hadn't slept through the night in ten years.

Public speaking amplified it. It began at a community center with creaky folding chairs and a podium that wobbled if you breathed too hard. Nathan's hands betrayed him with a small shake. He led with what would become his signature lines:

At twelve, my stepfather's abuse nearly broke me. I thought it made me weak. I was wrong. Survival forged a warrior within me—a warrior whose scars deserve recognition, whose healing demands urgency, and whose strength is no less because he was a boy.

A local reporter covered it. A regional nonprofit called. The *TED Talk "The Silent Epidemic: Why Male Survivors Matter"* crossed two million views, then three. Nathan learned to keep the talk taped to the inside of his bag, the pages softened at the edges.

Now, in the light of their new lobby, Sophia tapped the glass door with one knuckle. "Every time another man walks through here," she said, "I remember why we did this instead of taking the safer jobs."

Nathan nodded, thinking of faces. A forty-year-old man whispering, *"My wife hits me."* A teenager realizing his girlfriend's jealousy was control, not love. An eighty-year-old grandfather saying aloud, for the first time, what was done to him in the 1960s and watching his own breath hitch at the sound of it.

Janet, their receptionist, appeared with a clipboard and a half sleeve of colorful tattoos peeking out from her cardigan. "Mr. Parker? Your two o'clock is here—James Mitchell."

Nathan's jaw tightened a fraction. James Mitchell, thirty-nine, police department veteran. His intake notes were spare, as cops' notes often were. He kept his wedding ring on during sessions and stared at the floor when discussing injuries. "Knocked into a cabinet," he'd said once, rolling the words around as if they might shape-shift into the truth if he held them long enough.

"Also," Janet added, "three interview requests came in. And the National Coalition Against Domestic Violence wants to meet about a male-outreach pilot."

"Thanks," Nathan said and looked to Sophia.

She caught his eye and squeezed his hand—a silent *You've got him*—before heading back to her office.

James sat rigidly at the edge of the chair, hands cupped together as if he were trying not to spill something invisible. He was out of uniform—jeans, a gray sweatshirt—but the posture remained: alert, contained, scanning exits.

"How's your breathing right now?" Nathan asked after their check-in, keeping his tone easy. They'd learned not to start with words too big to carry.

James drew in air—shallow at first, then deeper. He nodded. "Better than last week."

"What helped?"

James thought for a while. "I left my radio at home," he said, almost surprised. "Could hear my own house for once."

Nathan watched his shoulders drop half an inch. "That's a good start."

Silence stretched, not unpleasantly. Nathan had learned to let silence do part of the work. It told a nervous system that no one would pounce; there was time.

James's eyes flicked to the window and back. "She...uh... threw my keys at me Tuesday," he said finally. He touched his temple. A yellowing bruise peeked beneath the hairline, thin as a smear of watercolor. He didn't point to it. He didn't need to.

"What happened right before?" Nathan asked, leaning back to keep the air open.

"I told her I was picking up an extra shift. She said I just didn't want to be at home. I said, 'Not everything is about you.'" He swallowed, jaw working. "Then the keys."

"Did you feel it coming?"

"Yeah." His mouth twisted. "But I didn't want to…I don't know…set her off."

They worked the scene as if two people were carefully unfolding a map. Where did his body first tell him danger was rising? ("Neck tight. Hands numb.") What tiny exits existed before it blew? ("Stand behind the island. Keep the doorway clear. Keep my voice low.") What might he say next time to keep the situation from escalating or to keep from feeding the fire? ("I'm going to take a walk. We can talk when we're both steady.")

When they'd sketched the safety plans, James's hands steadied. "I can stay with my brother two nights a week," he said. "He's got a couch. He won't ask questions."

"Okay," Nathan said. "Where will you put a go bag?"

James hesitated. "Trunk. She doesn't check the trunk."

"Good. And if you need me after hours"—Nathan slid a card across the table—"you leave a voicemail with the code word, and I'll know to call you back from a different number."

James took the card with both hands, as if it might break. His eyes were glassy but not spilling. "I'm tired," he said in a voice that belonged to a younger man. "I'm tired of pretending I can take it because I've seen worse."

Nathan let the words sit. He nodded once. "I don't think your body believes you can take it anymore."

James's mouth pressed into a line. Then he exhaled, and something in his posture let go—a half inch, maybe less, but real. They spent the last ten minutes practicing box breathing. Four in, four hold, four out. His shoulders rose and fell like a tide finding its pattern.

As the session ended, James stood, then paused. His gaze slid to Nathan's diploma on the wall, then to the photograph of a hiking trail Sophia had taken in the Adirondacks.

"Do you ever stop thinking about it?" he asked. "What happened to you?"

Nathan met his eyes. The question didn't feel invasive; it felt as if he were being asked to carry a corner of a couch. "I don't think *about* it all the time," he said. "I think *with* it. Some days it's loud. Most days it's background. It's quieter when I'm honest about what it was."

James nodded. His throat bobbed. "I'm gonna tell my brother," he said. "Tonight."

"That's a strong move," Nathan said. "Text me after you do. Just a thumbs-up so I know you're safe."

He walked James to the door. In the hallway, a janitor's cart squeaked by, the smell of citrus cleaner rising in its wake. James paused again, almost smiled, then left with his hands in his pockets, shoulders less squared for battle.

After James, the building settled into late-afternoon hush. Nathan returned to the lobby to find Sophia perched on the arm of a chair, sipping awful decaf from the staff machine and scrolling through photos for the website. She stopped on one of their group room—the circle of chairs, a throw blanket folded over the back of one, a tray of tea packets and plain biscuits on the side table.

"Do we look like a cult if we post this?" she asked, squinting one eye.

"Only the friendly kind," he said. He took the cup, winced, and set it down. "James is going to tell his brother."

Her eyebrows lifted. "That's big."

"Yeah." He rested a hand on the reception desk. "He noticed the moment his body told him it wasn't safe. That's new."

"Progress is noticing earlier," she said, and then—because she knew he would need to laugh—she shifted to a photo of their office plant, a stubborn ficus that had shed half its leaves in protest when they moved it. "We are losing this battle," she announced. "I read to it this morning. It dropped a leaf in response."

"Maybe it wants poetry," Nathan said. "Or a different therapist."

She snorted, slid her foot off the chair arm, and checked the wall clock. "Dinner at home? I can attempt that lemon chicken recipe that hates me."

"Deal," he said. "I'll set the smoke alarm to 'gentle encouragement.'"

They did a quick lock-check ritual—back door, side door, windows—and he took one last glance around. The room said, *You can breathe here,* without making promises it couldn't keep. He liked that.

The corridors were dim by the time Nathan finished a couple of late notes. He powered down his computer and stood with his palms flat on the desk, allowing himself thirty seconds of stillness. The silence wasn't empty; it hummed with a low contentment. *This is working,* he thought. *Not perfectly, but it's working.*

His phone buzzed in his pocket. Unknown number.

"Hello?"

A pause opened on the line. Nathan knew the shape of this kind of pause. It wasn't poor reception; it was performance.

"Hello, Nathan."

The voice came like a cold draft through a tight room.

"Richard," Nathan said, and his throat closed around the name. His hand tightened without choosing to.

"Nathan Parker, licensed clinical social worker now," the voice said, smooth as glass. "Impressive. I've been following your career."

"What do you want?" Nathan asked, already stepping away from the glass front of the office into the inner hall, an old instinct turning his back to the windows.

"To congratulate you. 'Champion of male abuse survivors.' Touching."

He glanced at the waiting room. The tree painting looked suddenly like a witness. "I'm hanging up."

"I wouldn't," Richard said lightly. "Not when I have something educational."

Nathan heard a faint clink on the other end, like ice in a glass, and his chest went tight. He kept his voice flat. "Say what you called to say."

"I've been thinking about our relationship," Richard said, letting the word *"relationship"* linger. "The story you've built your entire career on. And I realized…you never told the whole truth, did you?"

"I told the truth."

A soft laugh, the same one that had followed apologies years ago. "Did you? I've been talking to some of your clients. Marcus. David. James. They tell me very interesting things."

Nathan felt his stomach tip. He leaned against the wall and pressed his free palm to the paint as if the building could steady him. "You've been contacting my clients?"

"Mentoring them," Richard said. "Helping them see clearly. Marcus's wife isn't abusive at all—she's responding to his control. David's boyfriend has a very different version of events. And James"—Richard's voice warmed in false pity— "James embellishes. Men will admit a lot to someone who really listens."

Nathan pictured James's hands cupped as if he were holding water. He closed his eyes and saw the bruise at his hairline. "You're lying."

"Am I? Or is this crusade of yours not really about helping anyone—just about proving what happened between us was real?"

"It *was* real," Nathan said and heard the tremor.

"Was it?" The voice turned intimate. "I remember a troubled boy needing structure. Calling me Dad when he was scared. Hugging me after nightmares. You were grateful."

"I was a child," Nathan said. "You manipulated me."

"Or maybe therapy convinced you otherwise." Richard paused. "I have recordings, Nathan. Videos. You look very happy in all of them."

The room tilted a degree. Nathan's fingers went numb and then hot. He made himself breathe in for four, hold, out for four—James's exercise from twenty minutes earlier, borrowed now for his own lungs.

"Here's what's going to happen," Richard said, voice sliding back to business. "You'll close your little practice. Post a public statement about the dangers of false memory syndrome. Admit your childhood memories were distorted by suggestion."

"Never."

"Then I'll release the recordings. Publish a book. And I will dismantle every man you've helped. They'll be liars by the time I'm done."

A wash of nausea rose and broke. Nathan put his hand to the desk to ground himself. He looked at the thank-you card from Marcus—*For seeing me when I could not*—and at the group photo: eight men, shoulders slightly angled toward one another, the tentative geometry of trust.

"You have one week," Richard said.

The line clicked and went dead.

Nathan's breath came sharp, ragged. His fingers hovered over the desk, then found his phone. He hit his mother Angela's number.

She answered on the second ring. "Nathan?" Her voice was tight, urgent. "What's wrong?"

He pressed a hand to his forehead. "It was Richard. He called me. He knows about my clients. He—he says he has recordings. He wants me to close the practice, to say everything I remembered was false."

A long silence, then Angela's breath steadied into something firmer. "Listen to me. He's trying to rattle you. That's all this is—control, the same as always."

Nathan leaned against the wall, eyes shut. "What if he's telling the truth about the recordings? About Marcus, David, James…"

"No." Angela's voice sharpened. "You've done the work. You've helped them heal. I've seen it with my own eyes. He's twisting the narrative because that's what he does. You can't let him rewrite what you know is real."

Nathan's throat thickened. "He said he'll destroy everything."

"You've built something stronger than him," she said softly. "Don't let him inside your head. Not again. You can do this."

Nathan breathed out, the faintest thread of steadiness returning. "I can do this," he echoed.

Nathan stood very still. The room didn't move, but his insides did—a slow, disorienting slide, as if it were an elevator that overshot the floor and kept going. The clock on the wall ticked. Somewhere outside, a siren threaded the edge of hearing and then faded.

He reached for his phone to call Sophia. It buzzed before he touched it.

"Mr. Parker?" Marcus's voice tumbled out, breathless. "Something's happened. James Mitchell...he's...he's dead."

Nathan's mouth opened. No sound came.

"They're saying suicide," Marcus said, words scraping, fast. "But he told me a man came to see him yesterday. Said his name was Richard. Mr. Parker, I think we're all in danger."

Nathan found his voice. "Where are you right now?"

"In my car. Outside my apartment. I don't want to go in. Someone's been—" The line crackled with a startled curse. "There's a black sedan across the street, lights off. It's been there since yesterday."

"Marcus," Nathan said, steadying his tone the way he did in crisis calls, "drive to your brother's house. Now. Stay on the phone. I'm going to—"

A vibration against his palm cut him short. A text preview slid across his screen: "Unknown Caller."

He opened it.

One down. Six to go. Close the practice, Nathan, or watch them all fall. You have 48 hours.

—R

Attached was a photo of James's badge and service weapon, arranged carefully on a wood surface. The surface looked horribly familiar. Nathan's gaze snapped to his own desk.

The same knot in the grain. The same faint coffee ring in the upper left, barely perceptible unless you knew to look. He swallowed bile.

The phone buzzed again—another text, a link to an online burner account posting a draft statement about "false memories" with his name mocked up over it. His skin prickled. He became suddenly conscious of the building's quiet, of how the vents hummed, of the way the lobby's light reflected in the glass door as if a second door were layered over the first.

"Nathan?" Marcus's voice jolted him back. "I'm turning on Elm. I'm headed to my brother's. I— Wait." Tires squealed faintly on his end. "The sedan pulled out. It— Oh God, it's behind me."

"Go to a public place," Nathan said, moving now, keying open the back hall that led to the stairwell. "Gas station. Lights. People. Stay on the line. Do not go home."

He listened for the sound of Marcus's engine, for the exhale that would say he'd found light. His own breath went shallow, then deep, then steadied. A new text ballooned on his screen and popped with a soft chime.

Check the hallway camera.

—R

Nathan looked up. The tiny red LED above the exit door blinked. He hadn't noticed it blinking before.

He walked to the monitor in the staff room where hallway footage cycled through angles: back stairwell, break room, therapy wing. For a second, static washed the screen. Then an image resolved—grainy, monochrome. A man in a baseball cap stood at the far end of the corridor, half-turned, shoulders loose with the economy of someone who knew where he was allowed to be.

The time stamp said twelve minutes ago.

Nathan felt the exact moment his body said, *Danger.* It wasn't dramatic—just a narrowing, as if the air itself had stepped closer. He grabbed his satchel, patted for his wallet—present—and his keys—present—and checked the group room's door—locked. His brain began doing quiet math: *Where are the exits; what can become a barrier; whom do I call first?* He thought of Sophia's lemon chicken and of the ficus that seemed to resent poetry. The image was absurd and human, and it kept him from floating off the floor.

He texted Sophia, "Lock the house. Don't open the door for anyone. I'm on my way soon. Will call."

He hesitated and then added a heart. It felt like a small defiance.

Sirens began to thread the soundscape again—farther at first, then closer, weaving through lanes like something with a scent.

He dialed Sophia. It rang once. Twice. Voicemail. He hung up and tried again.

Nathan swallowed, then spoke after the tone.

"Babe, if anything happens to me, don't call my mom right away. With her health issues, we've got to make sure she doesn't take on too much stress. Promise me. I need you to promise."

Marcus's voice burst back in his ear. "I'm at the Speedway," he said. "Lights everywhere. The sedan turned off onto Maple. I think I lost it."

"Inside," Nathan said. "Buy gum. Anything. Keep the receipt. Text me a photo of the clerk if you can do it without—"

"I got it," Marcus said. "I'm going to my brother's after. I'll text you the address."

"Good." Nathan exhaled. "You did well."

"Mr. Parker?" Marcus's voice softened. "James wouldn't... I mean, he wouldn't just—"

"I know," Nathan said. "I know."

He ended the call before whatever lived behind his ribs pushed up into his throat. He needed to move. He needed to—

The front door to the office banged open so hard the glass rattled.

"Nathan Parker!" a voice shouted, amplified by the hard surfaces of the lobby. "Hands where we can see them!"

The hall filled with bodies—uniforms, drawn faces, the bright square of a body cam blinking like a small, impersonal eye. The sound crashed into him and kept coming—boots, clipped commands, someone on a radio giving the address and the word "secure."

Nathan's hands rose before he told them to. He turned slowly. The edges of the room sharpened to dangerous clarity: the grain of the desk, the scuff mark on the baseboard, the reflection of a red-and-blue flash spinning across the tree painting.

A detective stepped forward, badge on a chain, breath slightly winded from taking the stairs. "Nathan Parker, you're under arrest for the murder of James Mitchell. Turn around and interlace your fingers behind your head."

The words didn't make sense; they arranged themselves as sound and refused to fall into order. "What—" he started, then swallowed it. He could hear Sophia in his mind. *Don't argue. Breathe. Ask for a lawyer.* He interlaced his fingers. The cuffs clicked, cold and intimate on his wrists.

As the detective read rights that landed like hailstones, movement shifted in the hallway beyond. Nathan looked up…and there he was.

Richard stood back behind the cluster of officers, hands loose at his sides, eyes wide with concerned innocence. He wore the expression of a man trying not to intrude on grief. He had always been good at costumes.

"I tried to warn you about him," Richard said, voice pitched to the careful register people use in hospitals and churches. "Nathan's grip on reality has always been…tenuous. He's not a bad person. He just…" He let the end of the sentence trail off, generous in his restraint.

The detective glanced at Richard and then back to Nathan, professional neutrality bending, just slightly, toward a shape Nathan knew too well: *Maybe this explains things.*

Nathan looked at the group photo on his desk—change-makers, their shoulders angled toward one another as if bracing against a wind, finding a way to stand anyway. He wanted to tell them he hadn't failed them. He wanted to tell James he believed him. He wanted to tell Sophia everything fast enough that it still counted.

Instead, he swallowed, felt the cuffs press into bone, and said with careful breaths, "I want a lawyer."

They guided him toward the door. The evening had slipped darker while all of this was happening; the streetlights had come on like a row of eyes.

As they passed the lobby window, his own reflection slid across the glass and merged for a moment with Richard's in the hallway behind—two figures layered, one smaller inside the other, as if an old photograph had been laid over a new one. Nathan saw the boy he'd been standing on the landing outside a locked door, listening for footsteps.

He let the memory come and go without swallowing him. He counted his breaths—four in, hold, four out. He held the rope he had taught other men to hold.

Out on the sidewalk, air rushed his face with the bite of early evening. The cruiser's door loomed open, its interior light washing the back seat in a tired glow. Someone on the radio said, "Copy" and "ETA." The building's glass front reflected the patrol lights in red and blue, red and blue, a heartbeat that had lost its rhythm.

Nathan looked once more at the office—at the sign that still gleamed faintly where the paint was fresh, at the tree painting that now looked a shade more stern, at the polite pot of ficus that would drop another leaf tomorrow out of spite. He thought of James's careful breathing. He thought of Marcus's steadying voice at the Speedway. He thought of the men in that photo and of the boys they had been.

He had learned the shape of powerlessness early. He had also learned—slowly, stubbornly—how to survive it.

The door closed with a heavy sound, the kind that seemed to end a chapter all by itself. Richard stood by the steps with his hands folded as if he might pray. Nathan watched him through the glass, and for the span of a heartbeat, there was no sound—only the sight of a mouth curving into a small, private smile.

Nathan lifted his chin as the cruiser pulled away. He breathed in four, held, and breathed out again—steady, steady—already building the next step in his head.

He was not twelve anymore.

He would not be quiet.

And he would not break.

Chapter 13

DAY ONE
COUNTY JAIL

But, this time, survival wasn't enough.

The cell smelled of bleach layered over decades of rust, sweat, and something sourer that the bleach never fully erased. Nathan stepped inside, boots echoing once on the floor before the door slammed shut. The sound rang in his chest like a struck bell.

He closed his eyes and inhaled—four in, hold, four out. The same technique he'd taught his clients. *You are not twelve anymore*, he told himself. *You have tools. You have people who believe you.*

But the walls didn't care about his tools, and the cold metal bench didn't care about the truth. Here, he was just another body in the system—one with "murder" on his intake sheet.

A man was sitting on the lower bunk, elbows on his knees. He was wiry, mid-forties, tattoos blurred to a greenish blue. His gaze swept Nathan, not hostile, just assessing.

"What you in for?" the man asked.

Nathan's throat felt dry. "Murder," he said, the word tasting like rust.

The man whistled low. "You don't look like a killer."

"I'm not," Nathan said, meeting his eyes. "But someone dangerous wants everyone to think I am."

That earned a nod. "Tony," the man said, offering a callous hand. "County's a snake pit. Keep your head down, your back to the wall, and don't make promises you can't keep."

Nathan shook his hand. He knew the rules—different room, same survival.

That night, on the thin mattress that reeked of disinfectant and sweat, Nathan stared at hairline cracks in the ceiling. He counted his breaths against the shouts down the corridor and the slam of far-off doors.

During his childhood, when Richard's voice was the law and escape was impossible, he'd survived minute by minute. He called on that now. Hour by hour. Breath by breath. Heartbeat by heartbeat.

But, this time, survival wasn't enough.

This time, he planned.

Chapter 14

DAY TWO
SOPHIA'S INVESTIGATION

We're in this together.

Sophia sat in their home office, bathed in the cool glow of the laptop screen. The desk was buried under files, case notes, and printed emails—every scrap she could pull from Nathan's work with his clients who were survivors. Her search history over the past twelve hours looked like the beginning of a conspiracy theory:

> *Male domestic violence advocate dies by suicide*
>
> *Unsolved deaths—community leaders*
>
> *Richard Armstrong—criminal record*

The names piled up. The pattern emerged.

> *Dr. Michael Rodriguez, Phoenix—found dead in his office after threats about his advocacy work. Suicide, despite no history of depression.*
>
> *David Chen, Seattle—stabbed in a so-called "random mugging" days after testifying about male survivors.*

Marcus Williams, Denver—car crash, brakes failed the day before publishing a landmark study.

It was too much to be a coincidence. The line between them was jagged but real, and at the center, Sophia could feel Richard's hand.

Her phone rang. *"Dr. Jennifer Walsh."*

"Sophia," Walsh said without preamble, "Nathan mentioned Richard Armstrong months ago in a client-safety consult. I filed an ethics report. Nothing came of it. Now I wish I'd pushed harder."

"What did he tell you?"

"That someone from his past might target his clients. He didn't share details, but he was...afraid. Not for himself—for them."

Sophia's grip tightened. "Dr. Walsh, I think Richard's been targeting male domestic violence advocates nationwide. And I think Nathan's arrest is only the beginning."

The silence on the other end of the call was thick. "That's a hell of an accusation."

"I know," Sophia said, "but I'm going to prove it."

Her phone buzzed again before she could close the file. Angela's name lit the screen.

Sophia hesitated, then answered. "Angela?"

"What's going on?" Angela's voice was tight, frayed at the edges. "Nathan won't tell me much and I have not heard from him, and I can feel something's wrong. I need you to be honest with me."

Sophia pressed a hand to the desk, steadying herself. "I'm piecing it together, but it's bad. Richard isn't just after Nathan—he's been targeting advocates all over the country. People like him, people who fight for survivors. He's been arrested, but I am going to get him out."

A sharp inhale carried over the line. "My God."

"I don't have all the proof yet," Sophia said, "but I will. For Nathan. For everyone Richard's tried to erase."

Angela's voice dropped to a whisper. "Just...don't shut me out, Sophia. Not this time."

"I won't," Sophia promised. "We're in this together. I love you, mom."

Chapter 15

DAY THREE
THE BREAKTHROUGH

"We've got a problem."

Detective Maria Santos had seen every flavor of predator in fifteen years at SVU. But when Sophia Parker walked in with three boxes and a theory that made her stomach knot, Santos knew this wasn't going to be another routine case.

"You're telling me Richard Armstrong's been murdering domestic violence advocates?" Santos asked, flipping open a box.

"Not all advocates," Sophia said, sliding a folded timeline across the desk. "Men who work with male survivors. Every death came right before a breakthrough—testifying before lawmakers, publishing studies, national media coverage."

Santos's eyes moved over the dates and names. "Circumstantial," she said. "I need him at a scene."

Sophia pulled out her phone. "Richard sent Nathan a threat—James Mitchell's badge and gun. Look at the reflection in the badge."

Santos took a magnifier to the image. There it was—faint but clear. A man's face. Graying hair. Cold eyes. It matched the description Nathan had given of Richard.

"Son of a bitch," Santos muttered, "he caught himself in the evidence."

"There's more," Sophia said. "James's partner said he'd been paranoid, working on some personal investigation. He didn't say what."

Santos was already dialing. "If he left anything, we'll find it."

Sophia exhaled, her eyes drifting to the wall of case photos. Victims. Survivors. Missing persons. Somewhere among them, Nathan's life now hung in balance.

Santos lowered the phone. "We've got a problem," she said, her voice sharper now. "The warrant for Mitchell's effects just got flagged. Someone's already requested them."

Sophia's stomach dropped. "Who?"

Santos's gaze darkened. "Name listed as next of kin... Richard Armstrong."

Sophia's pulse slammed in her ears. "If he gets those, whatever's in there is gone."

Santos grabbed her keys. "Then we need to get there first."

As Santos and Sophia headed for the door, Santos's radio crackled.

"All units, be advised—incident reported at county jail, east wing."

Nathan's name came through the static, followed by words that made Sophia stop cold in the middle of the hallway: "Possible assault in progress."

Chapter 16

DAY FOUR
JAMES MITCHELL'S
FINAL GIFT

A quiet click. The door swung open.

James Mitchell's apartment was the picture of a man who lived by routine. The blinds were drawn halfway, casting even slats of light over a living room that smelled faintly of coffee and the faint tang of gun oil. Everything was ordered—mail stacked by size, jackets hung with military precision, boots lined up by the door as if ready for inspection.

In the bedroom closet, pressed shirts hung in a neat row. Behind them, tucked in the far corner, was a fireproof safe. Santos crouched, her gloved fingers spinning the dial before keying in the combination from the warrant.

A quiet *click*. The door swung open. Inside sat a single USB drive. White tape across the front bore two block-printed words: "Insurance Policy."

Santos carried it back to the station herself, resisting the urge to glance over her shoulder. In her gut, she knew this was it.

The files opened slowly on her computer, the blue loading bar crawling like a tease. Then they appeared—dozens of folders labeled by date. Photographs of Richard Armstrong shadowing men in different states. Audio clips, each labeled with a different alias. Handwritten notes scanned into PDFs.

Santos's heart rate ticked higher. The last file was an audio recording. She clicked Play.

Richard's voice came through first—smooth, confident, coiled with disdain.

"You see, James, the problem with you male domestic violence advocates is that you're all fundamentally weak. You've convinced yourselves that being a victim is noble, that admitting to abuse makes you brave. It doesn't. It makes you pathetic."

James's reply was measured but unwavering.

"You're recording this, aren't you? That's why you wanted to meet in person."

Richard laughed, a sound that made Santos's skin prickle.

"Even if you are, who's going to believe it? You're suicidal. I've spent months documenting your depression, your paranoia. Tomorrow, when they find your body—with Nathan Parker's fingerprints on the murder weapon—it'll just be another tragic case of a troubled man snapping."

"Nathan Parker never touched a weapon," James shot back. "You're framing an innocent man."

"Nathan Parker has been lying about me for years," Richard said. "Filling weak men's heads with excuses. Marcus Thompson could have been a real man if Nathan hadn't poisoned him with victimhood."

For twenty more minutes, Richard spoke as if cataloging his trophies—detailing how each advocate's death had been orchestrated, each "accident" engineered. His tone never wavered; this was a man reliving victories.

When the file ended, the office felt unnaturally still.

Santos called Sophia. "You need to get down here. We've got him."

Sophia arrived within the hour, hair pulled back in a quick knot, eyes rimmed red from lack of sleep. Santos hit Play again. Sophia's posture stiffened at the first sound of Richard's voice, her hands curling into fists on her lap. She didn't interrupt. She didn't cry.

When it ended, she exhaled sharply. "My God. He's been doing this for years...ever since he got out for what he did to Nathan and my mother-in-law."

Santos's mouth was a grim line. "This isn't just about silencing those on a mission to help survivors break free from the chains. It's about punishing men who dare to name their abuse."

Chapter 17

DAY FIVE
NATHAN'S RELEASE

"This is bigger than we thought..."

Nathan thought he was imagining it when the cell door swung open and Detective Santos stood there, paperwork in hand.

Four days in county had left its mark—hollowed cheeks, stubble shadowing his jaw, a stiffness in his shoulders from sleeping on a thin mattress under constant fluorescent light. His eyes had learned to track every movement in the pod, every sound in the hallway.

"Nathan Parker," Santos said, "you're free to go. All charges are dropped."

He blinked once, twice. "What?"

"Your wife…and James Mitchell," she said. "And a recording that will put Richard Armstrong away for life."

Processing was a blur of signatures, personal property bags, and the metallic snap of the cuffs coming off. As they walked toward the exit, Santos filled him in.

Nathan listened, the words washing over him—how James had been investigating Richard, how he'd documented everything, how he'd died with the evidence hidden away. When Santos mentioned the FBI, Nathan slowed. "The FBI?"

"This is bigger than we thought," she said. "Richard Armstrong—real name Marcus Reid—is wanted in connection with multiple across six states. All male domestic violence advocates."

Nathan stopped. "Multiple?"

"That we know of."

The front doors opened to a wash of afternoon light. Sophia was there before he could take another step, crossing the lot in a dead run. She collided with him in a hug so tight he had to catch his breath.

"I knew you didn't do it," she whispered into his neck. "But, Nathan…it's so much bigger."

They sat in the car, the engine idling, as Sophia told him about the pattern, the names, the years of killings. Richard hadn't just targeted Nathan; he'd been dismantling the movement one advocate at a time.

"He killed them because they were making a difference," she said. "Because they were changing minds."

Nathan stared out at the street, jaw tight. "Then we make the story louder."

He pulled out his phone, thumb hovering, then dialed. It rang only once.

"Mom?" His voice cracked, then steadied. "I'm out. I'm okay."

A sharp inhale on the other end. "Nathan—"

"It's all right," he cut in gently, though his pulse still thundered. "There was…a mistake. They realized the truth.

Sophia helped and found the evidence." His eyes flicked to the dashboard, to Sophia's reflection in the glass. "It's over— for now."

She was quiet, the kind of quiet that held both relief and unspoken terror.

"Please don't worry," he whispered. "I'm safe. We'll talk soon."

He ended the call before she could press for more, before his own voice betrayed the storm still clawing at his chest.

Chapter 18

SIX WEEKS LATER
THE INVESTIGATION DEEPENS

"This one's yours."

The FBI's field office conference room smelled faintly of burnt coffee and printer toner. Files and photos covered the table—names, faces, places, and crime scene images.

Agent Jennifer Morrison, a tall woman with sharp eyes, pushed a thick binder toward Nathan and Sophia. "Marcus Reid's been at this for over a decade. Multiple identities. Every move calculated to get close to male domestic violence advocates."

Nathan flipped open the binder. License photos under different names. Surveillance shots. Handwritten notes in a slanted script. "Why only men?" he asked, though he already sensed the answer.

Morrison tapped a page. "In his journals, he called male domestic violence awareness a threat to masculinity. In his mind, men who admitted abuse were eroding society. In his mind, advocates like you were the infection eating away at masculinity."

Sophia's hand closed over Nathan's on the table.

Morrison went on, her voice steady, "He wanted to erase the movement. And he nearly did."

Nathan's throat felt tight. "What were they working on? The men he killed?"

Morrison slid another file forward. "Rodriguez—conducting the first major study on male victims of female perpetrators. Chen—pushing for gender-neutral DV laws. Williams—developing a therapy protocol for male survivors of childhood sexual abuse."

Nathan read each page like a eulogy. Each death wasn't just a life lost—it was research halted, policy stalled, lives that would remain untouched by the help they'd been fighting to give.

Morrison hesitated, then pulled out a final file. "This one's yours."

The folder was thick. Two hundred pages.

"He's been planning your destruction for fifteen years," she said quietly. "Since you first spoke about your stepfather. He tracked your successes, your relationships, your vulnerabilities. This wasn't impulse—it was a long game."

Nathan didn't open it. He didn't have to. Sophia's hand tightened on his, grounding him in the here and now.

"This wasn't just about killing you," Morrison finished. "It was about dismantling everything you stand for."

Chapter 19

THREE MONTHS LATER
THE TRIAL

"Memory can be unreliable. Trauma is not."

The federal courthouse buzzed with an energy that felt almost electric. Reporters packed the hallways, cameras flashed in the marble lobby, and murmured speculation drifted through the air like smoke. This was no ordinary case. The press had dubbed it *"the most extensive domestic terrorism trial ever brought against a single individual targeting domestic violence advocates."*

Nathan waited outside courtroom 4B, palms damp despite the cool October air seeping in from the high windows. Exactly one year had passed since the first threatening call from Richard—Marcus Reid—and the symmetry of the date made his chest feel tight.

When the bailiff called his name, Nathan stepped forward. The walk to the stand felt longer than it should have, each step echoing in his ears. He placed his left hand on the Bible, his right raised, and swore to tell the truth.

As he sat, his eyes swept the gallery. Sophia and Angela sat in the front row, their gazes locked on him. Beside them was Dr. Walsh, calm but visibly tense. Detective Santos leaned slightly forward, elbows on her knees. Behind them sat Marcus Thompson and other male survivors from Nathan's group—shoulders squared, faces resolute.

He let the sight of them anchor him.

The prosecutor approached. "Mr. Parker, can you tell the court about your first encounter with the defendant, Marcus Reid, whom you knew as Richard Armstrong?"

Nathan took a slow breath. "The first time I met him, I was twelve years old. He was my stepfather. At that age, I didn't have the words for what he was doing to me. I just knew that the air in the house changed when he walked in. Every mistake felt fatal. Every compliment had teeth."

He spoke about the boy who learned to doubt his own memory, who thought every pain must somehow be his fault. The teenager who locked his feelings away so tightly it took years of therapy to pry them open. And, finally, the man who decided that his story would not end in silence—that his work would make sure no one else felt as alone as he once did.

"Mr. Reid didn't just abuse me as a child," Nathan said, his voice steady but edged with steel. "He spent decades trying to dismantle me…and every man I might help. He knew that silencing advocates meant male survivors would stay isolated."

The prosecutor nodded. "Thank you, Mr. Parker."

When the defense attorney rose for cross-examination, his steps were deliberate, his tone measured. "Mr. Parker, isn't it true that your memories of the alleged abuse are decades old? Would you agree that memory can be unreliable?"

Nathan met his eyes. "Memory can be unreliable. Trauma is not."

The attorney tried again. "And yet your entire professional identity is tied to being a survivor. Doesn't that give you a vested interest in portraying yourself as a victim?"

Nathan didn't look at the attorney—he looked straight at Reid. "My identity is tied to making sure other survivors don't end up dead, addicted, or hopeless. If telling the truth about my abuse threatens your client, that says more about him than me."

The defense attorney's jaw tightened. "You can't prove that your client—excuse me, *my* client—did what you say he did in your childhood."

Nathan reached for a sheet of paper from the evidence stack. "This is a transcript of your client's own words, from his recorded conversation with Officer James Mitchell. In it, he describes abusing me in detail. Would you like me to read them into the record?"

The attorney's objection was immediate and sharp, but the damage was done—the jury had seen Reid's calm expression twist ever so slightly.

The prosecutor stood for redirect. "Mr. Parker, in your professional opinion as a licensed clinical social worker, what was the defendant's ultimate goal?"

Nathan considered. "To keep male survivors invisible. Every man who speaks out gives permission for others to do the same. He believed killing advocates would keep us silent forever."

"And what happens when survivors stay silent?"

"Men die," Nathan said simply. "They die because they believe no one will believe them, because they think real men don't get hurt. Every advocate Mr. Reid killed represented thousands of men who might have found healing but never got the chance."

The prosecutor's final question was direct. "Do you believe the defendant succeeded?"

Nathan's gaze moved across the courtroom—the survivors, the advocates, the journalists scribbling every word. "No. He failed. Movements don't die with individuals. Every voice he silenced inspired ten more to speak. He tried to stop a movement. But movements are bigger than any predator."

Chapter 20

THE VERDICT
AND SENTENCING

The verdict came after less than four hours.

The verdict came after less than four hours. The jury filed back in, expressions unreadable. The clerk read the charges—eight counts of first-degree murder, conspiracy to commit murder, interstate stalking, witness intimidation, and domestic terrorism—and with each one came the same word: *guilty*.

Reid sat motionless, his hands folded on the defense table.

Judge Patricia Hernandez began the sentencing by addressing the packed courtroom. "Mr. Reid, your crimes were not simply against individuals. They were against the very idea that all victims deserve help and safety. You targeted voices that had already been silenced once, attempting to erase them forever."

Her voice never wavered. "You failed. Today, those voices are louder than they have ever been."

She sentenced him to life without the possibility of parole, plus two hundred consecutive years—"To ensure," she said, "that even in theory, you will never be free."

Reid's expression didn't change. The bailiffs moved to escort him out, shackles rattling. But just before he stepped through the side door, he turned his head toward Nathan.

His lips moved slowly, deliberately.

"This isn't over."

The words weren't loud, but they landed with the weight of a stone in Nathan's stomach. He felt Sophia's hand grip his tightly, grounding him in the now.

Outside the courthouse, the autumn air was crisp, the crowd buzzing with reporters' questions and supporters' relief. Nathan stood on the courthouse steps for a long moment before speaking.

"He wanted us silent," Nathan said to the cameras. "We're not."

Six months later, at the national conference, Nathan stood in the dim glow of backstage lighting, his hands loosely clasped in front of him, trying to steady the restless energy in his chest. Beyond the heavy velvet curtain, the cavernous convention center hummed with the low, steady murmur of over three thousand people. It sounded like the distant rush of the ocean, rising and falling in waves.

Somewhere out in that crowd were survivors who had carried their stories for decades. Policymakers who had written laws without ever meeting a male victim face-to-face. Journalists who had flown across the country to cover what they were calling a "historic moment for domestic violence advocacy."

The scent of fresh coffee drifted in from the lobby. The sharper tang of electronics—warmed microphones, cables, monitors—hung in the air around the AV booth just beyond the stage wings. Nathan could feel the subtle vibration of bass notes underfoot, a physical reminder of the massive sound system waiting to amplify his voice.

He had spoken at conferences before—hundreds of times, in fact. At trainings in cramped community rooms. On panels in university lecture halls. As the keynote speaker in hotel ballrooms. But this…this felt different. The stakes were higher, the crowd bigger, the purpose heavier. He could feel it pressing on his rib cage, the same way it had before court, before testifying, before moments that had changed the course of his life.

He glanced toward the side-stage monitor where the emcee was closing her remarks.

"…and now, please welcome to the stage a man whose courage, advocacy, and unyielding dedication have helped transform how we see and support male survivors of domestic violence. Ladies and Gentlemen, Nathan Parker."

The applause started as a polite wave, then surged into something more—thunderous, rolling, filling every corner of the massive space.

Nathan closed his eyes for a fraction of a second and inhaled. It wasn't the sound itself that gripped him—it was what it meant. This wasn't applause for him alone. It was for every man who had whispered his truth for the first time. For every survivor who had been told to "man up" and stay quiet, yet had spoken anyway.

He stepped forward into the lights.

The brightness hit him first—dozens of stage lamps cutting through the darkness, turning the audience into a faint blur beyond the first few rows. The podium stood at center stage, flanked by two giant screens projecting his name and image. As his eyes adjusted, he began to see the individual faces—reporters scribbling notes, survivors leaning forward, advocates gripping the hands of the people beside them.

And there, in the front row, Sophia. Her hand rested over the gentle curve of her pregnant belly, her face lit with pride and something else—an unshakable belief in him that had carried them both through storms. In seven months, their child would be born into a world they were actively trying to change. He gave her the briefest nod before he reached the podium.

He gripped the sides, grounding himself.

"Eighteen months ago," Nathan began, his voice steady but edged with the gravity of memory, "a man tried to convince me that my survival made me weak. That speaking out about abuse was shameful. That my life's work—helping men break free from violence—was dangerous."

He let his eyes sweep across the crowd. "He failed. But before he failed, he succeeded in silencing multiple voices. Multiple men who had dedicated their lives to helping male survivors find healing and hope."

The silence in the room deepened, the kind that seemed to have its own weight.

"Dr. Michael Rodriguez…David Chen…Marcus Williams… Dr. James Patterson…Robert Thompson…Dr. Anthony Martinez…Michael Johnson…and Detective James Mitchell."

He let each name breathe, resisting the urge to rush. These were not bullet points—they were lives.

"They died because they dared to challenge a narrative that has harmed male survivors for generations—the lie that real men don't get hurt. That admitting victimization is weakness. That seeking help is shameful."

Nathan straightened, his voice sharpening. "Today, I want to talk to you about a different narrative. A narrative about resilience, about courage, about breaking chains."

He leaned forward slightly. "One in four men will experience intimate partner violence in their lifetime. One in six will be sexually abused as children. These are not statistics—these are our fathers, our brothers, our sons, our friends. And yet, we've built a culture where their suffering is hidden, their stories untold, their pain minimized."

He let the words settle, then continued, "The chains that bind male survivors are forged not just by abusers, but by society itself. Chains of shame, silence, and isolation. But I have seen those chains broken."

Nathan's voice rose with conviction. "Real strength isn't enduring abuse in silence. Real strength is saying, 'This is wrong'—even when your voice shakes. Real strength isn't violence in return. It's walking away with your humanity intact. Real strength isn't hiding your pain. It's sharing it so someone else knows they're not alone."

He paused, and for a moment his mind drifted to Marcus Thompson. He saw him sitting in that cramped counseling room, hands trembling, voice cracking as he said for the first time, "I was abused." Nathan remembered the release in Marcus's posture, the way his shoulders dropped as if years of weight had finally lifted.

Returning to the moment, Nathan said, "Breaking these chains requires us to reshape our understanding of masculinity, victimization, and healing. It means creating spaces where men can speak their truth without losing their identity. It means believing without judgment, supporting without condition."

Then came the stories—expanded, vivid.

Dr. Michael Rodriguez had been on the verge of publishing treatment protocols that would revolutionize trauma therapy for men. Nathan described the afternoon he spent in Rodriguez's office, sunlight streaming across piles of annotated research papers, Michael talking with the same passion he used when describing his own recovery.

David Chen had been the policy warrior. Nathan recalled meeting him in a drafty state capitol hallway, coffee in hand, as David flipped through pages of legislative language, making the case for gender-neutral laws with the urgency of someone who knew lives depended on it.

Marcus Williams had been the researcher whose work was opening eyes across academia. Nathan remembered the night they stayed up until 3:00 a.m., debating how to dismantle flawed studies that had erased male victims from the data entirely.

Dr. James Patterson had founded the first residential treatment facility for male survivors of childhood sexual abuse. Nathan could still picture the converted farmhouse in Illinois, with its wraparound porch and therapy rooms that smelled faintly of cedar.

Robert Thompson had created the first university course on male domestic violence. Nathan spoke of sitting in on a lecture where Robert's students — men and women alike—leaned forward, furiously taking notes as if they'd been handed knowledge they never knew they needed.

Dr. Anthony Martinez had run support groups in Dallas that drew men from three neighboring states. Nathan described one such night—Anthony's voice steady, his eyes soft, as he told a room full of men, "You have the right to feel safe in your own home."

Michael Johnson had been the political connector, walking marble-floored hallways in DC, pressing for male-inclusive language in federal domestic violence legislation.

And Detective James Mitchell, who had given everything—his life—for the truth. Nathan told the audience how James's recorded conversation became the key evidence in Reid's conviction, how it became a rallying cry for survivors everywhere.

By the time Nathan finished, there were tears in the eyes of men and women across the auditorium.

He turned to the families in the room. "Believe your loved ones. Validate their experiences. Stand by them as they heal. Don't try to fix them—help them find the tools to fix themselves."

He faced the professionals. "Adapt your practices. Understand that shame, cultural stigma, and gender norms will shape how men disclose abuse."

To the policymakers, "Gender-neutral statutes. Equal funding. Law enforcement training that treats male victimization as real and urgent."

To advocates, "Every man you help find his voice carries forward the legacy of the men we lost."

Finally, his voice took on steel. "And to those who think male victimization is somehow less real, you are wrong. Domestic violence is not a competition. Pain is not diminished by the gender of the person who suffers it."

When he reached his closing, the words came like a vow. "The chains are breaking. The voices are rising. The healing has begun. And it will continue, one survivor at a time, until no one has to suffer in silence again."

The standing ovation was immediate, a physical wave of sound and movement.

Nathan stepped back, humbled, scanning faces—men crying openly, women gripping partners' hands, professionals nodding in quiet commitment.

Later, in their hotel room, Sophia handed him an envelope. "It's from the FBI. They've identified three more potential victims of Reid's network."

Nathan's jaw tightened. "The investigation continues."

"Are you ready for this to get bigger?" she asked.

He thought of Marcus Thompson, of James Mitchell, of the men whose names were etched into him now. "I'm ready," he said. "*We're* ready. Because this is bigger than us—it's about every survivor still waiting to break their chains."

They stood together at the window, city lights stretching to the horizon, knowing the work was far from over.

Chapter 21

CHAINS IN THE SHADOWS

Nathan Parker's life had changed again, but not in a way the world could see.

Nathan Parker's life had changed again, but not in a way the world could see. Marcus Reid was behind bars. The media frenzy had died down. Their nonprofit was growing fast, making headlines, reaching more male survivors than ever before. But beneath the surface, a quiet war still waged—against fear, against stigma, against the deep-rooted silence that domestic violence instills in men.

The morning after the national conference, Nathan sat alone in a small café tucked into a quiet Baltimore neighborhood. He stirred his coffee, but did not drink it. His hands were steady, but his mind spun like a carousel, one he couldn't get off.

A man approached the table. Early forties. Tired eyes. Broken posture. He looked as if he'd barely slept in weeks.

"You Nathan Parker?"

Nathan nodded, standing slowly.

The man stuck out his hand, hesitated, and pulled it back. "Name's Darren. I, uh…I came here straight from the shelter. They said you'd meet me."

Nathan nodded again, gently motioning to the chair across from him. "Sit down, Darren. Take your time."

Darren collapsed into the seat. "I feel like I'm suffocating just being in public. Like everyone can see what she did to me."

Nathan listened. That was what most survivors needed first—space to tell the truth.

Darren's story spilled out slowly. Married eighteen years. Two kids. His wife had started drinking heavily after her brother died. Then the yelling began. The hitting came next. Every punch followed by guilt. Every bruise hidden under shame.

He didn't leave because of the kids. Then, he didn't leave because he didn't think he could. Finally, he left because she beat him unconscious in front of their daughter.

Nathan didn't flinch. He just nodded. He'd heard these stories too many times. They were all unique, but painfully familiar.

"I don't want to press charges," Darren whispered. "I just want to stop waking up afraid. I want to be a dad my kids aren't ashamed of."

Nathan reached into his bag and pulled out a folded pamphlet. It wasn't a magic wand, but it was a start.

"This has a list of trauma-informed therapists. Male survivors. Specialized groups. And there's a lawyer on here who gets it. We'll cover the first few sessions."

Darren stared at the paper as though it were a lifeline. "Do people actually come back from this?"

Nathan nodded slowly. "You just did."

Chapter 22

FRACTURES

It started with the sound of a
plate shattering in the kitchen.

It started with the sound of a plate shattering in the kitchen. Sophia had dropped it—an accident—but Nathan was already against the wall, heart hammering, his breath caught between the past and present. He hadn't flinched like that in years. It wasn't just fear. It was the memory sewn into his nerves: a mother screaming, glass breaking, fists pounding.

Sophia approached slowly, arms out. "Hey, hey… It's just a plate, babe. I'm sorry."

Nathan closed his eyes, fighting to breathe, then let out a shaky laugh. "Yeah. Just a plate."

But they both knew it wasn't. It was a trigger. One of many. And now that the immediate danger of Reid was gone, the deeper war had begun—the war inside him.

He stopped speaking at panels. Stopped taking calls. The center kept running thanks to a strong team, but Nathan avoided the building. He couldn't explain it. Something about walking through those halls, passing rooms full of survivors… He felt like a fraud. As if the chain around his own neck were still there, tighter than ever.

He started therapy again. Not as a face of advocacy, but as a man barely holding on.

"Have you ever allowed yourself to feel angry?" his therapist asked.

Nathan stared out the window. "Angry at who?"

"Whoever needs it."

He wanted to scream. At his father. At Reid. At every judge who hadn't believed male victims. At himself.

Instead, he whispered, "I don't think I know how."

His therapist leaned in. "Then that's where we start."

The sessions unearthed years of silence. Not just what was done to him—but what it cost. The ways he performed wellness. How he wore strength like armor, even when his knees were buckling.

He began journaling. Long nights, ink staining his fingers. He wrote about the shelter, the basement, the sound of his mother gasping for breath. He wrote about the first time he saw a man cry and realized it was okay. He wrote about the dead men—James, Michael, David—and how he carried their ghosts with every step.

He also wrote about hope. The little boy who used to dream of escaping. The teenager who clung to books as though they were life rafts. The man who once believed healing was for other people.

Some nights, on the couch, he sat in silence with Sophia, their hands entwined. She didn't ask questions. She didn't push. That quiet presence saved him.

One day, he returned to the center.

He walked through the door and just stood there, breathing in the scent of old books and coffee. It felt as if he was coming home to a place he'd built but never truly entered as a survivor.

Angela was in the office, reviewing grant proposals. She looked up and smiled. "You're back."

He nodded. "I'm ready."

Not to save the world. But to let himself heal in it.

Chapter 23

THE QUIET ANCHOR

Until one evening.

The first time Nathan truly understood what peace could feel like, it wasn't in a therapy office or at the end of a speech—it was in the kitchen, hands trembling over the sink, when Sophia stepped behind him during a panic attack and said nothing.

Not because she didn't care.

Not because she didn't have advice or questions.

But because she knew.

She knew the language of silence, how it could be more than an absence of words—how it could be a shelter. In that stillness, he didn't have to justify his shallow breathing or explain why his grip on the plate was white-knuckled. He didn't have to fight against the shaking in his hands or the pounding in his chest. Silence became the air lock between chaos and safety.

Sophia had become the quiet force in his orbit, the gravity he hadn't realized was holding him together until the rest of the world's noise faded away. She didn't demand he be okay. She didn't expect him to wear his healing like a banner at every moment. She saw the journal pages torn and rewritten, the sleepless nights when his breathing came in sharp bursts…and she held space for all of it.

And that terrified him.

Real love, he'd learned, meant being seen. And when you'd spent most of your life hiding, being seen was not tender—it was terrifying.

So, sometimes, he ran.

Not in the literal sense, but in the quiet, practiced ways survivors learn. Dodging intimacy under the guise of late-night work. Claiming back pain and sleeping on the couch. Short, clipped replies at dinner. Eyes that never lingered long enough to risk being read.

Each time, Sophia didn't corner him. She didn't guilt him into talking. She stayed nearby but never suffocated.

Until one evening.

He was at the sink again, scrubbing a single plate long after it was clean, steam curling up into his face. Sophia padded in behind him, her footsteps soft against the hardwood, and slid her arms around his waist. Her chin found the space between his shoulder blades.

"Are you afraid I'll see something you don't want me to?" she asked, her voice low enough that he wasn't sure if she meant him to answer.

He froze. The answer was yes. What if she saw the parts of him still flinching, still waiting for the door to slam?

His shoulders went tight beneath her hands. She felt it.

"Because I already see it," she said quietly. "And I'm still here."

The words were heavier than any confrontation, sharper than any raised voice. He wanted to believe them, but belief had become a muscle he hadn't flexed in years—tight, resistant, painful to stretch.

He didn't turn around. Didn't respond. The fear lodged in his throat had been there too long, its roots tangled deep.

She pressed a kiss to his back and left the room without another word.

Hours later, he was on the porch, the night air cool against his skin. A mug of tea sat untouched beside him, the steam long gone. The yard stretched out in darkness, only the hum of crickets breaking the quiet.

Sophia slid the screen door open and joined him on the swinging bench. They rocked in silence until she spoke.

"I know you think you're going to break something good just by touching it."

His eyes stayed on the shadows beyond the yard. "Sometimes I don't even feel like a man anymore. I know it sounds ridiculous, but...after everything I've been through...everything I let happen to me...I feel like I failed at being one."

Sophia's fingers found his. "That's not weakness, Nathan. That's survival. You didn't fail—you endured. You protected the boy you used to be in the only way you knew how. You never gave up on him."

His voice broke. "I flinch when you raise your voice. Not in anger—just when you're excited. I hate that about myself."

Her thumb traced a slow circle over his knuckles. "I know why you do. And I'm not here to punish the reflexes your trauma gave you. I'm here to walk with you while you heal them."

He turned to look at her then, eyes glassy. "What if I never get it all out?"

"You don't have to," she said. "I'm not in love with your perfection. I'm in love with your honesty. Your fight. The way you keep showing up, even scared."

That night, Nathan made a call he'd been avoiding for months.

The next afternoon, he sat across from Dr. Lena Michaels, a woman in her sixties, whose sharp eyes didn't contradict the warmth in her voice.

"What brings you here?" she asked.

He didn't give her the polished version. Didn't talk about his credentials or the nonprofit. He told her the truth. "I'm tired of pretending I'm fine. I want to be able to be loved without bracing for impact." Saying it felt as if he were peeling off his own skin, raw and stinging.

Dr. Michaels nodded once. "Then let's begin."

They started with assessments, grounding exercises, and mapping the topography of his memories. But when Eye Movement Desensitization and Reprocessing—EMDR— began, nothing about it was gentle, nor was it meant to be.

The first target was the basement. The shouting. The sound of a plate breaking. The door slamming so hard it rattled the hinges.

"Hold that moment," Dr. Michaels instructed. "Now follow the light."

A bar of LEDs began to blink from side to side. Nathan's eyes tracked them, his breath shallow and uneven.

Then the sobs came—quiet at first, then shaking through his ribs.

Halfway through, another memory tore its way forward— one he hadn't planned to share.

He was ten years old, sitting cross-legged in his room while building a model car. The smell of glue and paint was sharp in the air. Footsteps thundered up the stairs, the door bursting open without a knock. His abuser's shadow filled the doorway.

"What are you doing?" the voice snapped.

Nathan held up the half-built car, trying to smile, but the words came like a blade. *"Waste of time. No one's ever going to care about anything you make."*

In the present, Nathan's throat tightened.

Dr. Michaels's voice was steady. "Stay with it. Follow the light."

The boy in the memory set the car down, hands suddenly clumsy. His chest ached with something he didn't have a name for yet—shame.

"What would you say to him now?" Dr. Michaels asked.

Nathan swallowed hard. "I'd tell him they were wrong. That what he makes, who he is—it matters."

The LEDs kept blinking. The breath he'd been holding released.

When Sophia picked him up afterward, she didn't ask what came up. She just took his hand in hers, her thumb brushing the back of it as they drove in silence.

In the weeks that followed, Sophia made subtle changes at home. She rearranged the bedroom so the bed faced the door—something Nathan hadn't realized he needed until the tension in his body loosened at night. She began narrating small actions before she did them. *"I'm walking into the kitchen now. I'm just setting this down here."* It wasn't condescending. It was her way of removing the land mines.

One afternoon, while folding baby clothes in the nursery, Nathan froze mid-fold. He held a tiny onesie against his chest, staring at it as if it might shatter.

"Do you ever feel like you're married to a broken man?" he asked, voice low.

The air in the room stilled. Sophia met his gaze without hesitation. "No. I feel like I'm married to a man brave enough to build something beautiful out of his brokenness."

That night, they lay together in bed, and Nathan cried openly onto her shoulder.

She didn't ask why. She didn't tell him it was okay. She just hummed softly, her breathing steady against his cheek until his own fell into rhythm.

By the sixth EMDR session, he no longer dreaded what would surface. He leaned into it. Each unraveled memory left more space inside him for something other than fear.

One day, they focused on a single sentence—words his abuser had drilled into him: *No one will ever love someone like you.*

Dr. Michaels paused the blinking light mid-sequence. "What would you say to your younger self in that moment?"

Nathan's voice cracked, but he said it anyway. "She was wrong."

The moment passed, but the shift remained.

When the EMDR cycle ended, he walked out of the clinic into sunlight so sharp it made him squint...and called Sophia.

"How's your heart?" she asked.

He tilted his head back to gaze at the sky. "Lighter than it's ever been."

Back at home, they stood in the baby's room, hands resting on the crib's rail. He spoke about lullabies and Saturday-morning soccer games. She teased about messy crafts and ballet recitals.

"I'm scared," he admitted.

"Me too," she said. "But we're not alone anymore. And that changes everything."

It wasn't perfect. It wouldn't ever be. But Nathan had stopped seeing his trauma as a disqualifier. He began to see it as a teacher. And Sophia—his quiet anchor—remained the harbor where the tides could crash without sweeping him away.

Chapter 24

THE WEIGHT AND THE WINGS

You survived. That's enough.
And now, you're choosing differently.

The small house rested under a quiet dawn, its windows catching the first fragile spill of sunlight. Outside, the horizon was painted in delicate shades of pink and gold, as if the night itself had blushed at being caught by morning. Inside, the air was still, the only sound the steady, soft rhythm of breath from the bedroom.

Nathan lay on his back, eyes half-open, letting the stillness settle on him like a blanket. For years, morning had been his most dangerous time—when the shadows in his head were thickest, when the body's instinct to wake came tangled with the memory of waking to shouting, to footsteps he'd learned to fear. But, today, for the first time in longer than he could measure, his body didn't jolt awake like prey. His eyes didn't dart to the corners of the room, scanning for danger.

Instead, he just…listened.

The faint rustle of leaves outside. The distant, tentative call of a mourning dove. Somewhere down the street, a neighbor's dog barking half-heartedly, as if even it couldn't muster much urgency this early. And beside him—the most grounding sound of all—Sophia's slow, even breathing.

It wasn't peace, not in the absolute sense. Nathan knew that peace wasn't something you woke into and kept forever. But something had shifted. The heaviness that had lived in his chest for years—an unmovable weight, like a stone slab—felt different. Not gone. But…softer. Manageable. He could take a deep breath without feeling as if it would break him.

It was a strange thing to feel his body leaning toward the light after so many years of curling inward against the dark.

He turned his head.

Sophia lay on her side, one hand curled loosely under her cheek, her hair spilling like dark silk across the pillow. Her face was still, brow smooth, mouth relaxed in sleep. She looked younger in the morning, somehow—as though the years had rolled backward while she dreamed.

Nathan's hand moved without thought, brushing a stray strand of hair from her cheek. His fingertips lingered, not out of necessity but because he wanted them to. Gratitude swelled in him, heavy and tender, almost too much to hold.

Her eyes opened slowly, catching his in that unguarded space between sleep and waking.

No words. Just that quiet, knowing gaze.

They had learned something together over these past months—sometimes words only dilute the truth. Sometimes presence is enough. Sometimes silence isn't an absence, but a kind of shelter.

Nathan's voice broke the stillness, softer than the air between them. "It's beautiful," he whispered, eyes flicking toward the sky outside.

A sleepy smile curved across her lips. "It is," she murmured, voice low and warm. "The world waking up. Just like us."

The phrase caught him—not just as something poetic, but as something true. He reached for her hand, threading his fingers through hers. His thumb brushed against her knuckle.

"I want to teach her," he said, and his voice caught halfway through. He had to push the rest out, slowly and carefully. "I want to teach her how to name her feelings. Before she learns to swallow them down, like I did."

Sophia's eyes softened, the way they did when she felt the weight under his words. "That's the greatest gift you could give her," she said. "To know herself. To be brave enough to feel."

Nathan looked away—not to hide, but because holding her gaze sometimes felt as if he were standing too close to the sun. Pride and fear braided together in his chest until he couldn't tell one from the other.

"I don't know if I'm capable," he admitted. "Some days I feel like I'm just…pretending to be okay."

Her hand found his face, palm warm against his skin. "You're more than okay," she said. "You're healing. And healing is messy. It's not in straight lines. But every day, you're moving forward."

The words slid into him like light through a crack. He didn't know if they would stay, but for now, he let them.

"I wish I'd known this sooner," he murmured. "Maybe I wouldn't have spent so many years fighting myself."

She gave his hand a squeeze. "You didn't know. You survived. That's enough. And now, you're choosing differently."

The memory was from eight years earlier. Nathan woke to a different kind of morning light—cold, gray, filtered through blinds that had been bent from too many slammed windows. His stomach ached with a dull, hollow gnaw that wasn't new. The shouting from the night before still clung to the walls. He'd learned to move quietly in those mornings, to keep the floorboards from creaking, to stay small.

Standing in the kitchen, he stared at the jar of peanut butter as if it were gold. The cabinet door was locked. Suddenly, his name was shouted once, sharp and short, like a warning. So he retreated to his room, hunger curling into his spine.

Back then, mornings had been a thing to survive.

The present returned with the warmth of Sophia's thumb tracing over his knuckles.

They got out of bed slowly, the day beginning with coffee and the soft domestic ritual of preparing breakfast in a shared kitchen. But the quiet between them held the weight of all they'd built to get here.

Later, as the sun climbed higher, Nathan drifted into the nursery.

The walls were painted a gentle yellow, the kind of color you couldn't assign a single name—soft gold in the afternoon, pale butter in the morning. The crib stood near the window, a mobile of paper cranes turning lazily in the faint breeze.

His hand skimmed the smooth wood of the crib rail, remembering the hours he'd spent sanding it down, wanting every surface to be safe, every edge rounded.

"I want her to grow up knowing her feelings," he said again, more to himself this time. "To give them a name. To not be afraid of them."

From the doorway, Sophia answered, "That's the kind of strength I want for her too. To know she can trust that love will hold her."

He turned, meeting her eyes. "You've always known how to hold me," he said, almost surprised at himself for saying it out loud. "Even when I couldn't hold myself."

"That's what love does," she said simply. "It stays...even when things break."

And then came the day everything shifted...

The day of the birth.

The house was quiet before they left, almost reverent. Sophia gripped Nathan's hand in the car, her face etched with determination and pain. He kept one hand on the wheel and one on her knee, his thumb drawing slow circles over the thin fabric of her leggings.

"You're doing great," he told her.

She managed a strained laugh. "You're white-knuckling the steering wheel."

"I've never done this before," he admitted.

"Neither have I," she said, softer now. "But I trust you."

Labor was long—sixteen hours of tension and release, of whispered encouragement and moments in which the room felt too bright, too loud. Nathan's voice never rose above a murmur as he counted her breaths, massaged her lower back, told her again and again that she was strong, that she could do this.

When Lila Grace finally arrived, the air in the room shifted. The nurse laid her on Sophia's chest, and for a moment, Nathan forgot to breathe.

She was so small. So impossibly small.

His eyes burned, tears spilling before he could stop them. He touched her cheek with one trembling finger, afraid to press too hard, as if she might dissolve under his hand.

"I was right," he whispered. "She was worth the wait."

Sophia, pale but radiant, looked up at him. "So were you."

The days that followed blurred into a rhythm both relentless and tender. Night feedings, diaper changes, the quiet miracle of watching Lila's chest rise and fall in the dim light.

Nathan found himself sitting in the nursery at odd hours, holding her against his chest, feeling the fragile weight of her and the strange grounding power in it.

One night, he whispered into her downy hair, "I didn't grow up with a father. But I'll hold you every chance I get. Not just with my arms—with my heart."

From the doorway, Sophia watched, silent tears sliding down her cheeks. Her hand rested on her own belly, feeling the faint flutter of their second child.

When Nathan finally looked up, he said quietly, "She's so small. What if I mess this up? What if I become him?"

Sophia stepped into the room, placing her hand over his. "You're already the father she needs. And you're healing too. We're all healing—together."

That night, after Lila was asleep, Nathan carried her into the living room and sat in the rocking chair. The lamplight wrapped the room in gold.

"I don't know what kind of man I'll be for you," he whispered to her sleeping face. "But I promise I'll try every day to be someone you can trust. Someone who stays. Someone who listens."

Her tiny hand curled around his thumb, and something inside him loosened.

He pressed a kiss to her forehead. "Your voice is stronger than they know. And I'll help you find it, no matter what."

As he rocked her, Nathan understood—healing wasn't erasing the past. It was carrying it differently. And as he looked down at his daughter, he felt something inside him unfurl.

Nathan stayed in the rocking chair long after Lila's breathing deepened into that slow, even rhythm babies seem born knowing. Outside, the wind whispered against the siding, a gentle reminder that the world was moving on out there, but in here…everything had stopped.

Her weight against his chest felt as if it were the most fragile and unshakable thing he'd ever held.

And then, without warning, a memory surfaced.

He was six, sitting on the floor in front of the old radiator in his grandmother's living room. The metal rattled and hissed, breathing out waves of heat that wrapped around him like a secret. She had made him cocoa—too sweet, the marshmallows already melting into a white foam on top. He remembered the sound of her humming in the kitchen, a song without words, just melody.

For years afterward, he had trouble remembering what safety felt like. But that cocoa, that hum, that warmth—those were the only times the air didn't feel as if it might turn sharp at any second.

Lila shifted, made a small, squeaky sound, and resettled, bringing Nathan back to the present, where he still sat in the rocking chair.

He had forgotten that memory until now. Nathan felt something in his chest shift—not in pain, but in the strange relief of remembering he had once known warmth.

And maybe that was the point—not to pretend the pain hadn't happened, but to find the places where light still managed to leak in. To give those moments to her, over and over, until they were the rule and not the exception.

Sophia padded in quietly, her hair loose, her sweater sleeves pushed up. She knelt beside the chair, resting her hand on Lila's tiny back.

"What are you thinking about?" she asked.

"That I want her to remember mornings like this," he said. "Not because they were rare. But because they were constant."

Sophia smiled faintly, leaning her head against his arm. "She will. You're making them constant."

––––––––––––

Days blurred into weeks, weeks into months. There were moments Nathan stumbled. Nights he woke sweating, certain he'd heard footsteps that weren't there. Days he withdrew into himself without meaning to. But he always came back.

Because there was no going back to the man who measured love by its absence.

––––––––––––

Two years before meeting Sophia, Nathan sat in his car outside a community center, gripping the steering wheel until his knuckles went pale. Inside, a support group for male survivors was starting. He had never gone. Had told himself he didn't belong there.

But, that night, he'd thought about the boy he used to be—small, hungry, listening for footsteps in the hall—and realized that no one had come for him then.

If he didn't go in, if he didn't speak, that boy might keep waiting forever.

So he opened the door and stepped inside.

The sound of Lila stirring pulled him back to the present. She blinked up at him, her expression unfocused but content, and something in him anchored.

"You're why I went in that room," he murmured. "I just didn't know it yet."

The kitchen smelled like pancakes and syrup. Lila, now five, sat at the table with her feet swinging wildly above the floor. Her curls were tied up in a lopsided ponytail, the kind Nathan had learned to make by watching videos on his phone.

"Daddy," she said, holding up a crayon drawing, "this is us."

He took the paper carefully. Stick-figure Nathan, tall and smiling, stood beside a smaller Lila wearing a yellow crown. Between them was a big red heart, and underneath, in wobbly letters, she had written, "LOVE MEANS STAYING."

Nathan swallowed hard. "Who taught you that?"

"You did," she said matter-of-factly, pouring more syrup onto her pancakes.

Sophia, standing at the stove, glanced over her shoulder with a quiet smile. She didn't have to say anything.

Nathan set the drawing on the counter, knowing he'd keep it forever.

That night, after Lila was asleep, Nathan stood in the doorway of her room. The night-light cast a soft glow across her face. She was breathing evenly, one hand curled under her cheek—just like her mother.

Sophia came up behind him, slipping her arms around his waist. "She's happy," she whispered.

"I think she knows she's safe," he said.

"She knows because you show her every day."

Nathan exhaled slowly, the weight of years settling differently in his chest—not as a burden, but as something weathered.

"I used to think healing was about forgetting," he said. "Now, I think it's about building something stronger in its place."

Sophia rested her head against his back. "We're building it. All of us."

Nathan closed his eyes, letting the truth of that sink in. This small house, this family, this life—they were not accidents. They were the result of every hard choice, every moment he'd decided to try again instead of turn away.

The night outside was quiet. But, inside, something powerful was unfolding—a kind of revolution that didn't make noise, that didn't need to.

And as he stood there in the doorway, watching the steady rise and fall of his daughter's breathing, Nathan understood that his promise to her had already begun to take root.

The cycle had stopped here.

He would keep showing up—every day, every year—until love was the only inheritance Lila ever knew.

Chapter 25

THE RECKONING

But something had shifted.

The nightmares had returned with a vengeance.

Nathan woke in a cold sweat again, the phantom smell of blood and broken glass clinging to him as if it were stitched into his skin. Richard's voice still echoed in his head—jagged, unhinged—right before everything shattered.

But something had shifted.

The nightmares didn't own him anymore.

He sat up in the quiet dark, chest rising too fast, eyes scanning the shadows out of habit. Outside, the wind moved through the trees—not a voice, not Richard. Just wind. Just the present.

Still, peace felt like a trick. Like the calm before something cruel.

He padded toward the kitchen, each floorboard groaning like a reluctant witness. The cold wood grounded him just enough to remember he was awake.

Angela was already there, her hands wrapped around a mug of tea as if it might keep her from unraveling. The steam curled against her face, but her eyes were far away.

"I had the dream again," Nathan said, voice low. The words breached the dam he'd built inside himself. Speaking them felt dangerous, as though the nightmare could bleed into daylight...but keeping it inside was worse.

Angela's gaze flickered. "Me too."

They let the quiet hold them. Not the comfortable quiet they'd shared once upon a time—this was the heavy, breathless kind, the kind you only share with someone who's been through the same war.

"I thought I understood trauma," Angela said after a long pause, her voice roughened by honesty. "I thought counseling survivors meant I knew the terrain. But I never knew what it felt like to be trapped...until Richard."

Nathan studied her. How could something so broken between them still ache with love?

"You're not trapped anymore, Mom."

Her mouth twitched in something that might've been a smile. "No, but some days I still feel the shackles. Invisible ones."

The sun was only beginning to stain the sky purple when Nathan asked, "Do you ever think about confronting him? Not in court. Just...us."

Angela hesitated, thumb tracing the rim of her cup. "Sometimes. But people like Richard...they don't hear you. They twist you." Her chest tightened at the thought of sitting across from him again. *I will not let him own another second of my life,* she told herself.

"Still," Nathan pressed, "I need him to know what he destroyed."

"Then maybe," Angela said softly, "it's not about him at all. Maybe it's about you."

Three weeks later, Kate—their attorney—sat across from them, fingers steepled. "I can arrange it. Supervised. Controlled. But you need to be ready. He will try to get inside your head."

"We're ready," Nathan said, though a small voice inside him wasn't sure.

The room was cold, stale, and windowless—built to strip the world away until only truth or lies remained.

Richard was brought in shackled at the wrists and ankles, yet he moved as if the chains were ornamental. His eyes landed on them, slowly and deliberately, his mouth curling into a smirk that hadn't aged.

"Well," he said, voice slick as oil, "the prodigal son...and the martyr."

Angela felt her stomach flip but kept her expression still.

Nathan gripped the edge of the table until his knuckles blanched.

Richard leaned back, studying them like pieces on a board. "I've been thinking, you know. About how things went wrong. About how maybe...we could've fixed it if you hadn't been so dramatic."

Nathan's mind snapped to the basement. He was twelve years old, standing barefoot on the cold concrete, the smell of mildew thick in the air. Richard's shadow stretched over him.

"If you'd just kept quiet, none of this would have happened."

His nails dug into the table. "Stop."

Richard ignored it, eyes narrowing as if he were a predator testing a cage. "You used to look up to me, Nathan. Remember? You wanted to be strong. I tried to teach you, but—"

Angela's memory surged. She was kneeling on the kitchen floor, sweeping shards of a broken plate, while Richard loomed over her.

"Look what you made me do."

Her hands had bled that night, but she'd kept sweeping.

Angela's pulse spiked. "We're not here for your version of events."

Richard's smirk sharpened. "You think you can define me with your little speeches?"

"No," Angela said, voice steady now, "we can't define you. But we can define what you did. To me. To my son."

Richard laughed once, bitterly. "Always the victim."

"And you," Nathan said, leaning forward, "will always be what you are. But you don't get to live in my head rent-free anymore."

For the first time, Richard's gaze flickered.

Angela stood, her chair scraping against the concrete. "You don't own us. Not anymore."

Nathan rose beside her. "You'll tell yourself you won today, that you got under our skin. But you didn't. You can't. We came here for one thing—to leave lighter than we arrived."

Richard opened his mouth, some venom forming, but they turned before it could land. The chains clinked when he shifted, but his words stayed behind, unspoken.

Outside, the air was sharp and clean. The sun had just broken through the clouds, spilling light like a quiet blessing.

Angela inhaled deeply. This time, the breath reached the very bottom of her lungs. She hadn't realized how long she'd been breathing shallowly. Tears slipped down her cheeks, but they were different now—hot with release, not grief.

Nathan stood beside her, staring at the distant horizon. For a long time, neither of them spoke.

Then Nathan said, "It's strange. I thought I'd feel...bigger after that. Stronger."

Angela looked at him. "You don't have to feel bigger. You just have to feel free."

The words landed somewhere deep inside him. He realized his shoulders weren't tight anymore; his jaw wasn't clenched. The silence between them felt different too—not the silence Richard had weaponized, but one they owned together.

They walked slowly toward the parking lot, each step feeling less like escape and more like arrival. At the car, Angela rested her head briefly against Nathan's shoulder.

"You did good in there," she murmured.

"So did you."

When they drove away, neither looked back.

The sun followed them through the windshield, lighting the road ahead—bright, unbroken.

And for the first time in years, the silence between mother and son felt like peace.

Chapter 26

THROUGH THE FIRE

Freedom was not a single triumphant moment.
It was a thousand quiet choices
made in shadows.

Freedom was not a single triumphant moment. It was a thousand quiet choices made in shadows.

It was Angela waking in the night, heart racing, only to realize there were no footsteps in the hall.

It was Nathan stepping outside without scanning every shadow.

It was learning how to laugh again without guilt.

Healing was messy. Some days shone with light; others dragged with the weight of an anchor called memory.

Angela returned to therapy—not as a counselor, but as a patient. The first time she sat across from Dr. Jennings, she felt the odd sting of role reversal. *I've told survivors this exact thing,* she thought, *but I've never admitted it to myself.*

One rainy afternoon, her voice cracked. "He made me feel like I was nothing. Even when I knew, I didn't know how to leave."

Dr. Jennings took her hand. "That's because abusers sever your connection to yourself. Survival becomes your only language."

Angela's tears blurred the room. "How do I forgive myself for letting Nathan live through it?"

"You start by understanding that you *saved* him, even in the moments you didn't know how," Dr. Jennings said softly. "You survived...and now you're living."

Nathan, too, began therapy again. He talked about the silences, the shadows in the corners, the rage at Richard, at his mother, at himself.

After one grueling session, he found Angela on the porch at sunset. He sat beside her without a word.

"I keep thinking about what could've happened if you hadn't stopped him that night," he finally said.

Angela took his hand. "I know. I think about it too."

"I hated you for a long time," Nathan admitted. "I thought you didn't see it. But maybe part of me was scared—scared of what would happen if you *did*."

Angela's eyes shone. "I was scared too. But I'm not anymore."

Nathan smiled faintly. "Me neither."

Chapter 27

RESILIENCE

Years passed.

Years passed.

Richard stayed in prison, his letters unopened and discarded. His power over them had shriveled into dust.

Nathan graduated with honors, his joy returning like breath after a long dive. He formed a band with friends who understood invisible wounds.

Angela traveled to schools and shelters, telling her story—not as a therapist, but as a survivor. Her memoirs, *Quiet Thunder*, became a lifeline for many.

But the real victories weren't on stages.

They were in the warmth of their kitchen, in the echo of shared laughter, in the ability to sit in silence without fear.

One autumn evening, they sat in the backyard watching stars.

"Do you ever think about what we survived?" Nathan asked.

Angela nodded. "Every day. But I also think about how far we've come."

The stars seemed brighter now, no longer dimmed by waiting for footsteps behind them.

"You saved me," Nathan said.

"No," Angela whispered, "*you* saved *me*."

Nathan leaned back, thinking. "I want to start a nonprofit. For kids like me—a place they can go when home doesn't feel safe."

Angela smiled. "That's beautiful."

"I want to name it after Dad," Nathan said quietly. "For the good memories…before everything changed."

Angela's hand went to her heart. "He'd be proud."

Nathan nodded. "And so am I…of us."

Chapter 28

THE SOUND OF TWO CRIES

Even now, Nathan couldn't shake the question:
Why there? Why them?

They hadn't heard a knock—only the faint scrape of wicker against wood. When they opened the back door, the night air rushed in, cold and sharp, and there he was: a baby in a basket, swaddled, silent, the chill clinging to his skin. Not the front porch, where neighbors might notice, but the hidden threshold no one used. Even now, Nathan couldn't shake the question: Why there? Why them?

Tucked beneath the blanket had been a single sheet of paper, the handwriting jagged and rushed. *"Take care of him. I can't anymore."* It was signed only with a name: Mei. And beneath it, almost as an afterthought, one more word: Luke.

The wails started just after midnight—sharp, wet, unyielding. They carved through the quiet like a blade.

Nathan sat in the dark nursery, rocking slowly, the old chair creaking beneath him. His hoodie hung open, bare chest pressed against the tiny, trembling body in his arms.

Luke was sweating. His cheeks were hot, but there was no fever. No rash. Nothing outwardly wrong—except the raw panic that refused to leave his voice. The sound was different from colic. Lila had wailed from stomach cramps; this was deeper. Primal. The kind of cry that came from losing something you can't name.

Babies remembered in their bodies, didn't they? The way a room smelled, the warmth of certain arms, the rhythm of a heartbeat. Luke's body knew these weren't the arms that had carried him for seven weeks. His mother's scent, the cadence of her breath—gone. And this stranger, this man with tired eyes and an unsteady heartbeat, was trying to take her place.

Nathan's mind kept circling back to the same thought. *He knows she's gone.* And maybe that was for the best. Mei's face had surfaced before, once in the local paper, twice on the evening news. Headlines that blurred together now: neglect, police calls, a child nearly taken before the case fell apart. Sophia had pulled the clippings from her searches, laying bare what the whispers in town already knew.

"Shh… I know," Nathan whispered, rocking forward and back. "I know you don't know me. I know she's not here."

He pressed his forehead against Luke's, the heat of their skin mingling. Sweat dripped down Nathan's neck. His own body was tight with exhaustion and the old fear he thought he'd buried—the fear of not being enough to keep someone safe.

When the baby's cries reached a pitch that made his skull throb, Nathan tried something else. No lullabies. No "Twinkle, Twinkle."

He began to sing one of his own songs—an old one written back in college, before life had taken its sharper turns. Minor sevenths, slow phrasing, raw and imperfect. The kind of song that came from someone who knew about loss.

At first, nothing. But then the cries faltered, breaking into hiccups. Luke shifted against him, cheek finding the hollow of Nathan's shoulder. His fists unclenched.

And then…silence.

In the hallway, Sophia stood barefoot, hair messy from sleep, Lila's warm weight slumped against her shoulder. She had been heading to check on them, but stopped when she saw Nathan like this—eyes closed, still rocking, a stranger's child asleep in his arms as if they'd known each other forever.

She didn't speak until Luke's breaths evened out. "I think," she whispered, "we're already in it."

Nathan kept his gaze on the sleeping boy. "Yeah," he said quietly, "we are."

Chapter 29

TRIAGE

Nathan felt something shift inside him—not quite relief, not quite fear. Maybe both.

The days that followed blurred into a loop of bottles, burp cloths, and two babies on mismatched sleep schedules.

Nathan kept music playing in the background—soft fingerpicking, quiet folk loops—so the house wouldn't feel like a hospital.

Sophia hung blackout curtains in the nursery.

The air smelled faintly of formula and lavender baby wash, and there were moments, in the thin sunlight of late afternoon, where it almost felt normal.

Almost.

They hadn't called DCF yet. Every conversation about it ended the same way: "What if they can't trace Mei or take her history seriously?" Sophia asked and Nathan countered, "What if they do and give Luke back to *her*?"

The unopened DCF form stayed in the kitchen drawer. Nathan's laptop sat on the counter, a browser tab open to the "Report a Found Child" page for days without a single key pressed. They were in survival mode—triaging like in an ER. Today's crises first. Tomorrow's decisions…tomorrow.

On a gray, rain-smeared afternoon, Nathan leaned in the doorway while Sophia bathed Luke in the bathroom sink. She was quiet, methodical—cupping water over his chest while murmuring words Luke probably didn't understand but leaned toward anyway.

Finally, Nathan asked the question he had been holding in since the first night. "What if no one shows up to claim him?"

Sophia didn't look up. Her pause was long enough to be an answer in itself.

When she finally spoke, her voice was low but certain. "Then I guess…we claim him."

Nathan felt something shift inside him—not quite relief, not quite fear. Maybe both.

Chapter 30

THE VISIT

They didn't have to wait long.

They didn't have to wait long.

The social worker came on a Tuesday morning, her arrival announced by three sharp knocks and the sound of rain on her umbrella. Her name was Darlene, and she had kind eyes framed by crow's feet…but her clipboard made it clear kindness wasn't her primary job here.

From the moment she stepped inside, the questions came in steady, practiced tones:

"How did you find the baby?"

"Why didn't you contact emergency services immediately?"

"Have you ever completed any foster parent or trauma-informed care training?"

Every question felt like a trip wire. Nathan sat straighter on the couch, Luke balanced in his lap, answering carefully, measuring his words so none could be twisted against them.

Sophia brought out mugs of tea neither of them touched.

Darlene examined Luke gently, checking his skin, his reflexes. She glanced at Lila too, noting the way she eyed the stranger but stayed near her parents. She asked about support systems, finances, emotional strain.

Nathan felt sweat pooling under his collar. Every answer felt as if it might decide the boy's fate.

When the questions finally stopped, Darlene closed her folder with a quiet click. "You'll hear from us," she said, standing. "But I'm not going to recommend removal at this time."

Sophia exhaled so sharply it almost sounded like a sob. "Thank you."

Darlene's face softened, but her words didn't. "Don't thank me yet. He's not yours—not legally. Until then, you're just the place he was left."

It stung.

When the door closed behind her, the house seemed quieter than before. Nathan turned toward the living room, where Luke and Lila lay side by side on the play mat—two sets of tiny fists, two pairs of wide eyes watching the same spinning mobile above them.

"She's wrong," Sophia murmured.

Nathan nodded slowly. "Yeah. He wasn't just left here."

He looked at the boy, so new to their lives but already altering its gravity.

"He came home."

Chapter 31

THE UNWRITTEN DAYS

Love doesn't always knock loudly.
Sometimes, it taps.

Weeks passed.

They learned each other's rhythms like a language—morning feedings in sync, double stroller walks to the park, shared playtime on the living room rug. Sophia found herself humming lullabies again, realizing halfway through that she was inventing them, each melody stitched together from the sound of Luke's tiny laugh.

When they got Luke baptized, Mei's first letter was tucked inside his keepsake box. The Parents line on the certificate was left blank. That blank space ached, but it also told the truth.

A few weeks later, another letter arrived—forwarded through a domestic violence advocate. Mei was still hiding. Still healing. Her words were steady this time: *"If he's happy, keep him. If he's loved, let him stay loved."*

The day the adoption papers were finalized, Nathan sat on the floor with his guitar. Luke clapped offbeat while Lila danced in circles. Sophia tried to sign the forms without her tears smudging the words. Both pens were chewed at the ends—Sophia's signature mark. Nathan's hand trembled as he wrote, a mixture of awe and disbelief tightening his chest.

This is forever, he thought. The name on the page anchored Luke to their story.

Luke Parker.

Three syllables that shifted the center of their world.

Sophia laughed through tears at the messy signatures, the ordinary chaos framing an extraordinary moment. *We're really doing this*, she thought—not just legally, but with her whole heart.

That morning, Sophia snapped a photo: Nathan lying in a blanket fort, Lila curled on his chest, Luke nestled under his arm, babbling into the air. She captioned it: *"All my heartbeats in one place."* They framed it.

When Lila asked years later, *"When did Luke come to us?"* they answered only, "He arrived when we were ready." The rest of the story belonged to them.

Some families are born. Others arrive on a doorstep.

They chose him.

And he, in turn, chose them—soft eyes, tiny hands, full trust.

Love doesn't always knock loudly. Sometimes, it taps.

Age four...

One spring afternoon, Luke followed Lila into the backyard, determined to keep pace. Nathan watched from the porch as Luke's little legs pumped harder than they needed to.

Lila slowed down without making a big show of it—just enough for him to catch up.

When Luke tripped, Nathan instinctively stood, heart thudding. But Luke popped up, brushing dirt from his knees with a stubborn little scowl.

That night, Nathan carried him upstairs. Luke's head rested on his shoulder, warm and heavy. "Did you get hurt today?" Nathan asked.

"No," Luke said, "I just fell."

Nathan smiled in the dark. He knew the difference between falling and being pushed. Luke did too.

Age eight...

Rain hammered the roof as Nathan folded laundry in the living room. Luke sat nearby, building a lopsided LEGO tower. Out of nowhere, Luke asked, "Was she scared?"

Nathan froze. "Who?"

"My first mom."

Nathan set the laundry down. "Yes. But not of you. She was scared of what the world might do to you. She didn't know if she could stop it."

Luke stared at the tower for a long time before whispering, "That's why she gave me to you."

"She didn't give you away," Nathan said gently. "She chose a future for you. One where you'd be safe."

Luke nodded, but Nathan could tell he was turning the words over like stones in his hands, searching for the smoothest way to hold them.

Age ten, in the attic...

Nathan found him cross-legged on the attic floor, a cardboard box open before him. Baby clothes. Family photos. And at the bottom—folded gently—Mei's original letter.

Luke's voice was quieter than usual. "Can I keep this in my room?"

"Of course."

Nathan watched him carry it as if it were made of glass.

Age sixteen, the letter...

On his sixteenth birthday, a letter came from Mei. She had found them through a legal contact, asking only for their mailing address. She'd waited this long so as not to interfere, but she wanted to wish him a happy birthday, to thank Nathan and Sophia, and to tell Luke she was okay.

Luke read it alone in his room. Then he walked downstairs and placed it on the table.

"I want to meet her," he said.

Sophia reached for Nathan's hand.

"We can write back," Nathan said. "Ask if she's open to that."

Luke nodded. "I just want to know where I came from. Not because I don't love where I am. Just...because both things can be true."

They met in a park halfway between two cities. Mei wore a simple blue dress and a pendant necklace. Her hands shook until Luke reached forward and held them.

"Hi," he said, "I'm Luke."

Her smile broke into tears. "You've grown so much."

They talked for an hour—about books, music, dreams, her story. No accusations. No apologies. Just presence.

Before parting, Mei hugged him. Not long. Not desperately. Just enough.

"Thank you for growing," she whispered.

Luke whispered back, "Thank you for letting me."

The night before graduation...

Luke sat on the front steps with Nathan, watching the stars.

"She still writes," Luke said. "Every few months."

Nathan nodded.

"She calls you my dad."

Nathan's throat caught. "Is that okay with you?"

"It's perfect."

Luke hesitated. "I think I want to do what you did. Not just take people in—but make a space. A place where the left-behind kids feel seen."

"You'll be amazing," Nathan said.

"I want to name it after her—*Mei House.*"

Nathan closed his eyes. "She'd be honored," he said, though some part of him feared she might have seen too much of Richard in him.

"I hope so."

Nathan pulled him close. "You made us a family, Luke. We didn't just save you. You saved us."

Years later...

Nathan sat alone on the same porch where it all began. The wind rustled the trees, an old lullaby. Fireflies blinked lazily across the yard.

Sophia stepped out with a steaming mug. "Hot cocoa. Extra marshmallows."

He chuckled. "Medicinal."

Inside, Luke and Lila were cooking—badly. Pots clanged. Someone laughed. The sound of a house still full.

Sophia looked toward the door. "They've grown so fast."

"They've grown kind," Nathan said.

She smiled. "Do you ever think about the note?"

"Every day."

"What if we hadn't opened the door?"

Nathan's voice was steady. "Then the best part of our story would've never happened."

The screen door creaked open. Luke leaned out, apron stained with sauce. "You two gonna help, or just have a nostalgic porch moment?"

Lila's voice followed. "We're burning the bread again!"

Sophia kissed Nathan's temple. "Duty calls."

As they stepped inside, the porch light flickered gently in the breeze.

Beneath it, a faint etching remained carved into the wood: *"Love knocked. And we let it in."*

Every family has a beginning.

Theirs began with a knock.

A letter.

And a child whose name meant light.

And in that light, they found not only each other.

But themselves.

Chapter 32

LIGHT BETWEEN THE SHADOWS

Nathan knew, every day, the only mistake
would have been closing the door.

It's strange, Nathan thought, *how a new life can arrive in your home without permission from your plans. Stranger still how quickly the days can bend around it.*

Once, there had been a rhythm—frantic but familiar—around Lila's feedings, Sophia's anxious midnight checks, Nathan's guitar looping softly in the background.

Now, there were two rhythms overlapping like poly-rhythms in a jazz piece—one baby fussing just as the other was soothed. A constant call and response. It was a music only exhausted parents knew.

January brought a quiet snow, the kind that slowed the world without asking. Sophia stood by the window in her robe, a chipped mug cupped in her hands. Flakes drifted past the glass, soft and endless, layering the yard in white.

Luke—now four months old—slept against her chest in a navy wrap, his breath warm against her collarbone. Lila, beads of drool at her chin, sat on the rug, stacking wooden blocks, then knocking them down with the gleeful violence only toddlers possess.

"You ever think about how lucky we are?" Nathan's voice broke the silence as he padded in from the hall, hair wild from sleep, sweatpants low on his hips.

Sophia glanced over, a small, tired smile tugging at her lips. "I do. Not often enough."

He set his coffee down beside her and looked out at the snow. "We could have missed all of this—this life—by changing our minds that morning."

She didn't answer in words. Instead, she shifted Luke's blanket up over his ears and exhaled slowly.

Nathan stepped in close, pressing his cheek to her temple, their breaths syncing. "Even on the worst days?" he murmured.

"Especially then."

Resilience, he thought, *isn't always about grand gestures. Sometimes it is surviving another sleepless night, choosing to show up when you felt empty, forgiving yourself for not being the mythical "real parent" you thought you were supposed to be.*

Outside, the snow kept falling. Inside, soft lamplight painted the room gold. Sophia hummed a lullaby she didn't remember learning.

Nathan found his songs shifting—melodies slower, chords warmer, hope stitched into every note.

Even when problems felt unsolvable—jobs on the edge, money thin, case manager forms collecting dust—their home still made space for joy. For an hour or two at a time, they could forget the paperwork and just live in the noise of Lila's laughter.

The blocks toppled, and Lila squealed.

Luke startled, his lip trembling—then laughed at the touch of Sophia's fingers.

Some families are born of blood. Others are born of a single merciful choice. Nathan knew, every day, the only mistake would have been closing the door.

Chapter 33

THE WAITING

Life still rolled forward.

DCF's silence grew heavier with each passing week. Nathan called twice. Sophia called once, her voice shaking in a way he hadn't heard since the early days—back when advocacy was a fire in her chest and not a daily drain. They left voicemails, sent polite but pointed emails, checked the mailbox like clockwork.

Life still rolled forward.

Luke came down with his first fever. Sophia hovered over the crib, thermometer in hand, whispering comforts he couldn't understand but leaned into anyway.

Lila, seeing her brother's red cheeks, crawled in beside him with her favorite bear, tucking it under his chin. Somehow, the gesture calmed him more than medicine.

At the pediatrician, a nurse glanced at the chart and frowned. "So...Parker. You're not the biological mother, right?"

Sophia stiffened.

Nathan's fingers found hers. "She's his *real* mom," he said, steady and sure.

The nurse blinked, cheeks coloring. "Sorry, just paperwork confusion."

But the damage was done.

Later, in the car, Sophia broke. "I'm scared they'll take him away, Nate. I'm scared every day."

He gripped the wheel hard. "They won't. And if they try—we fight."

It was strange—staking a claim on a child who'd come to them in crisis. But the love was real, fierce. The kind that kept you awake more from worry than from crying.

Sophia began writing in a blue notebook—a journal for Luke. First smiles. First tastes of puréed carrot. First night without tears. She never showed Nathan, but he saw the way she carried it room to room, always within reach.

Nathan poured his feelings into music. His songs shifted from loss to finding—lyrics about arrival, belonging. Some nights, Lila joined in, pounding her toy drum in chaotic harmony.

Luke's eyes always found Nathan when he played, his tiny body swaying to the sound.

The months unfolded in small rituals—baby yoga at dawn, movie nights with subtitles so they could hear over baby noises, rainy-day baking sessions with flour dusting the floor. The waiting was still there, a quiet shadow, but joy learned how to slip past it.

Chapter 34

LITTLE FEARS, FIERCE JOYS

The drive home was quiet.

It was Sophia's idea to take a family photo.

They drove out to the country on a Saturday in April, windows down to let the spring air whip through the car. The road curved past farms and through a field where the grass stood waist-high, tipped in gold by the late-afternoon sun.

The photographer laughed with them, catching moments between poses. Lila stomped in the grass, curls catching the light. Luke stared at the clouds as if he'd just discovered the sky. Sophia's hair tangled in the wind, and Nathan reached out to smooth it, his fingers lingering on her cheek.

Halfway through, Lila's hair clip vanished. Tears came hard and fast. Sophia's eyes glassed over too—it was always the smallest things that cracked you open. Nathan crouched, brushing dirt from Lila's knees. "It's okay," he said. "Real life. That's what I want in the picture anyway."

The shutter clicked: Sophia cradling Lila, apology in her eyes; Nathan holding a drooling, half-asleep Luke; all four of them pressed together, imperfect but whole.

The drive home was quiet. Lila fell asleep clutching Sophia's hand. Luke gurgled softly in the back seat. The only sound was the hum of the tires and Sophia's low, instinctive humming.

That night, Nathan scrolled through the shots. He stopped at one where Sophia was mid-laugh, Luke tugging her hair, Lila's smirk tilted between pride and mischief. He set it as his phone background. Every glance at it reminded him why they kept fighting.

Sophia printed a copy for the fridge, pinning it beside Mei's letter. Each morning, she touched both. "We're here," she whispered. "We're still here."

Chapter 35

THE LETTER BOX

*She felt—at the same moment—an old ache and
something startlingly new: relief.*

It took months. But, finally, the letter arrived.

Not the thick packet of legal papers they'd been rehearsing for, the ones that would mark "Adoption Day" in bold on the calendar. Instead, it was a simple white envelope—creased from its long journey—forwarded by the caseworker, no return address.

Sophia turned it over in her hands, her thumb brushing the faint ridge of the seal. It was lighter than expected, as if it carried only air. She slit it open carefully, afraid of tearing whatever lay inside.

A card slid out, painted with delicate watercolor bluebells, the brushstrokes soft and imperfect, as if they'd been made in a moment of stillness.

The note inside was short. Each word looked carefully chosen, as though written and rewritten in someone's mind before ink ever touched paper.

Dear Sophia, Nathan, and Lila,

I think of him every day, but less in sorrow now, and more in hope. I wanted you to know that. I wanted to thank you for letting him be loved, not for what he's lost, but for all that he is.

With gratitude—

Mei

Sophia read it once.

Then again.

Then a third time, her fingers trembling.

She felt—at the same moment—an old ache and something startlingly new: relief.

For months, she had built invisible defenses in her mind, rehearsed impossible conversations in the shower, in traffic, in the seconds before sleep. *What if Mei asks for him back? What if she changes her mind?*

But the letter wasn't a summons or a goodbye. It was permission—quiet, enormous permission—to go on loving Luke without the shadow of a courtroom hanging over them.

Nathan appeared at her side. She handed him the letter without speaking. He read it in silence, then closed it gently and walked to the living room. There, he knelt by the wooden keepsake box where Luke's first blanket, his tiny hospital bracelet, and Mei's original note were stored. The new card joined them, tucked carefully between layers of memory.

And then, without planning to, they both cried—messy, shoulder-shaking sobs that felt as if they were unclenching fists they hadn't known they'd made.

It was grief. But it was also release.

Chapter 36

AFTER THE WAITING

Choosing something hard, they realized,
didn't mean they couldn't also choose joy.

The months that followed felt lighter. The waiting hadn't disappeared—it never would—but the sharp edge of uncertainty dulled. Nathan and Sophia began to see themselves not as placeholders in Luke's story, but as permanent lines in its pages.

Choosing something hard, they realized, didn't mean they couldn't also choose joy.

Nathan started playing at a small café on Thursday nights, the air warm with the scent of espresso and the hum of conversation. Sometimes Sophia brought the kids. Lila danced in front of the stage with sticky hands from a shared muffin, while Luke cooed in Sophia's lap, eyes fixed on Nathan's guitar as if it held the secrets to the world.

Sophia returned to work part-time that spring. On her first day back, she cried the entire drive to the office, the empty car seat in the rearview mirror feeling like a missing limb.

At her desk, her phone buzzed.

It was a photo from Nathan—Lila and Luke in their high chairs, faces smeared with yogurt, both flashing exaggerated thumbs-up. The caption read, *"All good here. Go be amazing."*

She smiled, wiped her cheeks, and opened her laptop.

At night, Sophia would lie beside Lila until her breathing slowed, brushing curls from her forehead. Down the hall, Nathan rocked Luke, the low hum of his voice seeping through the walls.

For so long, survival had been the measure of success. Now, they were learning how to live.

Chapter 37

THE QUESTIONS CHILDREN ASK

The first question came on a quiet morning, sunlight pooling on the kitchen floor.

The first question came on a quiet morning, sunlight pooling on the kitchen floor.

"Why's Lukey mine?" Lila asked, clutching his soft bear in one hand.

Sophia, caught mid-sip of coffee, crouched down so they were eye level. "Because he's your brother. He's ours. Just like you."

Lila tilted her head. "But...where's his other mommy?"

Sophia hesitated—not because she didn't know what to say, but because she wanted to get it right. She smoothed her daughter's hair. "His other mommy loved him very much. But she needed to make sure he was safe. So she brought him here, where we could all love him too."

Lila blinked, then broke into a grin. "He's lucky. He gets two mommies!" And just like that, she ran off, problem solved.

That night, when the house was quiet, Sophia told Nathan about the exchange.

"Do you think we should tell her more?" she asked.

"There'll be more questions," Nathan said, taking her hand. "And there'll be more answers. But for now? She knows about love. That's enough."

Sophia dreamed that night of Mei—not her face exactly, but the sense of her—walking away, down a sunlit road, at peace.

Chapter 38

SCHOOL DAYS, NEW FEARS

"Don't go."

Time doesn't slow for anyone, least of all parents.

By autumn, Luke was old enough for pre-K. The first morning was chaos—sandwiches made, socks mismatched, Nathan buttoning Luke into a blue windbreaker while Sophia tied Lila's shoes.

At the classroom door, Luke hesitated. His small fingers curled around Sophia's leg, his voice barely above a whisper. "Don't go."

Sophia knelt until her eyes met his. "I'll be right here at the end of the day. I promise."

He nodded, but the goodbye stuck in her chest like a splinter.

Through the glass door, they watched him sit in the circle, eyes darting back every few seconds to check that they were still there. When he finally joined the other kids in building a block tower, Sophia let out a breath she hadn't realized she was holding.

That afternoon, he ran into Nathan's arms with a paper rocket clutched in his hand. "I made this!"

"Looks like it could reach the moon," Nathan said.

Lila insisted they tape it to the fridge the moment they got home. "Next time," she declared, "we ALL make rockets."

Sophia laughed, the ache in her chest replaced by something steadier—certainty.

Chapter 39

SEASONS TURNING

There's enough love for everyone.

They built their life in seasons.

Spring meant planting basil and tomatoes in the garden, even though only half the seeds took.

Summer meant beach days, sandy feet, and Luke burying Nathan's toes in the surf.

Autumn storms sometimes knocked the power out. They'd light candles, tell stories, and make shadow puppets against the walls.

Winter brought snow forts, cocoa with extra marshmallows, and cookie decorating that left more sprinkles on the table than on the cookies. Nathan played guitar; Sophia sang along softly.

Every year, near Luke's "gotcha day," Nathan would take him for a walk at dawn.

One year, Luke asked, "Will Mei ever visit us?"

"Maybe someday," Nathan said. "And you can miss her and love her at the same time. There's enough love for everyone."

Chapter 40

LILA'S STORY AND NEW NAMES

May your light never dim.

The family's story became part of Lila's schoolwork when she was nine.

For a writing assignment titled *"The Story of My Family,"* she wrote *"My Brother Came in a Basket."* The pages were filled with her own brand of logic and love. She wrote about "the day our hearts opened up super wide" and drew a giant yellow sun over their house.

When her essay won a local prize, Sophia framed it.

Luke—now reading it—stopped to trace the drawn sun with his finger. "That's us—the wide heart."

The adoption ceremony was small—friends, a judge, and a representative from Mei's advocate circle.

Nathan's voice trembled as he read their vows. "We promise to give you roots and wings, to honor your past, and to always choose you."

Luke smiled shyly, sensing only that something important had just been promised to him forever.

Mei's absence was felt, but her presence was there in the yellow lily she'd sent. The card read:

For Luke—May your light never dim.

Afterward, Sophia whispered, "He wasn't left behind. He was loved forward."

Chapter 41

MILESTONES

*They became a quiet ritual, folded into
the rhythm of their lives.*

Each year, a new letter arrived from Mei. Sometimes they contained stories, sometimes only a few lines.

They became a quiet ritual, folded into the rhythm of their lives.

At ten, Luke asked to read them all. Sitting beside the box near the living room window, he worked through each one in silence.

"Was she scared?" he asked finally.

"Yes," Nathan said, "but she was brave too. Brave enough to make sure you'd be safe."

"Can I write back again?"

"Anytime, just like last time, buddy."

They wrote together, slipping in a photo of the four of them at the beach.

Time stretched forward, and childhood unfolded in a thousand ordinary ways.

The years were full—field trips, scraped knees, piano recitals, soccer games.

Luke found music; Lila found maps and dreamed of travel. They argued, forgave, and sometimes stayed up past midnight sharing snacks on the porch.

Every birthday, Sophia baked a cake too big, and Nathan insisted they sing off-key.

The family wasn't defined by the day Luke arrived anymore. They were defined by everything they'd chosen to build since.

Adolescence brought harder questions, questions the letters alone could not answer.

At thirteen, Luke found Nathan in the living room, guitar in hand.

"Do you ever...feel like I'm your son? Even though I wasn't supposed to be yours?"

Nathan set the guitar down carefully. "It's not just a feeling, Luke. It's the truth. Every day, every choice we've made—that's family. And I will always choose you."

Something eased in Luke's face, and when Nathan pulled him into a hug, the boy didn't pull away.

Chapter 42

RETURN OF SPRING

They spoke of music, books, dreams.

Years drifted—middle school, first heartbreak, discovery of poetry. Lila became a budding artist; Luke leaned into music. Sophia built a garden; Nathan ran his nonprofit, helping kids find safe havens of their own.

Their family, once fragile and improvised, had become rooted and unworried. Friends entered their orbit, drawn to laughter and a feeling of belonging.

In her journal, Sophia wrote:

Joy grows here. Even after pain. Especially after pain.

When Luke was sixteen, Mei reached out with an offer. She lived a few hours away and was teaching at a community center.

Luke wanted to go. He told Nathan and Sophia over warm croissants one Sunday, "It's not because I'm not happy— I am. I just need to see where I started. To say thank you."

Sophia squeezed his hand. Nathan nodded.

The meeting was quiet, heartfelt. Mei was older, her eyes wiser, but her smile the same as the one Nathan remembered.

They hugged—awkward at first…then real. They spoke of music, books, dreams.

Mei confessed she followed every update. "Even just a whisper from your family reached me."

When they returned home, Luke placed a photo of Mei and him on his bookshelf. For the first time, his two worlds felt twined together, not separated by trauma, but joined by choice.

Chapter 43

THE DOOR IS ALWAYS OPEN

Their lives didn't close like a book;
they unfolded like chapters still being written.

Their lives didn't close like a book; they unfolded like chapters still being written.

Luke went off to college and majored in psychology, inspired by Sophia's courage.

Lila traveled, sending postcards from every new place.

Nathan and Sophia grew older, savoring their house full of echoes and memories.

On the night of Luke's graduation, the family sat on the porch—side by side, shoulder to shoulder.

"Was it worth it? All the risk?" Lila asked.

Sophia scrutinized her grown children, then smiled. "Every second. Because loving you is the story I'll never get tired of telling."

A breeze. The porch light flickered.

On that warm night in Boston, Nathan realized that, all those years ago, what mattered most was not how the story began, but how they had chosen—over and over—to let love in.

Chapter 44

SCARS AND LAMPSHADES

When things hurt, he fidgeted, turned inward.
Never using your hurt as a weapon—but never
hiding it away as a shameful secret, either.

Nathan learned young that pain had a silence to it. Throughout his twenties, into fatherhood, he carried it like a lamp covered with a heavy shade—sometimes its illumination glowed, sometimes it waned, but the shape of the lamp never really changed. Only the way he chose to see its light.

He learned that he did not have his mother's habit of stoicism. When things hurt, he fidgeted, turned inward.

When Sophia once asked him, early in their relationship, "What's really wrong?" he'd joked, "I'm fine. I'm the king of fine." But, deep down, he hated how much he wanted to be rescued and how hard it was to ask for help.

The most important thing therapy taught Nathan—years after Richard, years after becoming Luke's father—was that vulnerability is not the pain itself. It is the willingness to look at pain without flinching or running away.

He learned to listen to the trembling at the edges of his voice. He learned to speak the "afraid" out loud, first to Sophia, then to Lila when she herself was little and learning the word, and finally to Luke, who always seemed to test the lock on every door in their house, metaphorically and literally.

Fatherhood forced Nathan to see himself as both a protector and a survivor—which was not a contradiction, as he'd once thought. He did not have to deny the hurt to raise a child; he had to face it and give his children something softer, safer, freer.

He learned—not overnight but gradually—that it is okay to wake up anxious. That real bravery is making breakfast anyway, hugging your son tightly, going to therapy. Never using your hurt as a weapon—but never hiding it away as a shameful secret, either.

The lamp stayed. But the shade grew thinner, the room brighter.

Chapter 45

REPAIR, OVER AND OVER

It took just a spark.

Nathan had grown up believing that apologies were rare currency in a family—only offered after something catastrophic occurred. And in Richard's house, even that currency was counterfeit. If you upset Richard, you fixed it. If Richard upset you, you still fixed it. Angela's apologies were whispered olive branches meant to reset tension just enough for everyone to breathe, never to actually repair.

That winter, the air in their own house was ragged with coughs and the metallic scent of cold medicine. Small bodies shuffled in socks from couch to kitchen. Sleep deprivation lay across the rooms like a fog—thin in places, dense in others.

It took just a spark. Nathan bent over the counter, trying to get soup into bowls, while the kids squabbled somewhere behind him. A sharp crack in the air—his own voice, raised without meaning to, pitched with a hard edge he didn't intend.

Lila froze mid-step. Eyes wide, her small frame began to tremble before tears blurred her vision.

Luke didn't say a word—he slid his small hand into Nathan's, his grip steady but asking, *What just happened?*

In their faces, Nathan saw his own seven-year-old self—stomach tight, pulse pounding, searching a room for sudden danger.

I never wanted to be this man.

He stepped out into the hallway, stared at the wallpaper until it blurred, forehead pressed to the cool wall. He counted backwards from fifty, each number an anchor, willing the adrenaline down just enough to return without the storm.

When he stepped back into the room, the light had shifted—late afternoon bleeding into the blue edge of evening. He dropped to his knees so they could see his eyes.

"I'm sorry," he said softly. "I shouldn't have yelled. It wasn't your fault."

He unpacked the moment in simple, clear words, afraid that anything more complicated would dilute the truth.

Lila folded into his chest, sobbing into the fabric of his shirt.

Luke's fingers clenched tighter around his.

Repair didn't bowdlerize the hurt. But it planted something in its place—trust, the kind that grows stubborn roots after being offered water during a drought.

That night, after the kids had gone to bed, he stood in the doorway of their bedroom. "I lost my temper," he told Sophia. He let her see the ugly, tired, trying parts of himself.

She didn't offer reassurance. She simply said, "Thank you for apologizing."

Nathan learned—the hard way and then the honest way—that repair is the cornerstone, not a mere footnote, when building a family. The homes constructed on "I'm sorry" and "I forgive you" are the only ones where real love knows how to live.

Chapter 46

YOU PARENT THE CHILD, NOT YOUR FEAR

"That's okay. You loved her."

The worry never fully left him. As Luke grew, Nathan feared he would pass down invisible things: the twitch at sudden noises, the impulse to withdraw, the self-questioning that gnawed. He feared he would give them hurt as if it were an heirloom.

One sunny spring afternoon, when Luke was twelve, Nathan found him sitting in the backyard under the budding maple. Knees drawn tight to his chest, cheeks blotched, the boy's hands clasped around his knees. Beside him, a small, still shape in a shoebox—the pet rabbit he'd doted on for two years.

Nathan's chest tightened. His instinct flared: Smooth this over; talk about the circle of life; crack a joke. Do anything to pull that look off his son's face.

Sophia's hand landed lightly on his forearm. "Let him feel it," she whispered. "Don't steal the lesson."

So Nathan lowered himself onto the grass beside Luke. They sat there, wind moving the young branches overhead, silence stretching but not suffocating.

"You really miss her, huh?" Nathan said at last.

Luke nodded, tears tracking slowly down.

"It hurts a lot," Nathan said. "That's okay. You loved her."

He said nothing more…and did not try to reach for the tear to wipe it away. Sometimes, he realized, the bravest thing wasn't rushing to heal, but trusting that your child could stand in their own storm and still find their way home.

Chapter 47

MAKING PEACE WITH THE PAST

But children have a way of bringing the past into the present.

For years, Nathan had run—from memories, from vulnerability, from the belief that his only inheritance was damage.

But children have a way of bringing the past into the present.

One evening, Luke, now a teenager, asked about Mei, about adoption, about "where I'm from." The question was casual enough, tossed out over the clink of dinner plates, but it opened a door Nathan had barred instinctively for years.

He felt a hitch in his breath, old pain shifting in its sleep deep inside him.

He wanted his answer to land clean, free of the bitterness that had once been his default. So he looked his son in the eye and spoke plainly. "She loved you, but she had to leave. That's not about your worth. I loved my mother even when she was trapped. People fail us. And we can still build something good."

It startled Nathan that he actually believed these words as he said them.

He learned that real peace wasn't pretending the shadows weren't there; it was standing in the midst of them with the light on and telling the story candidly. That way, his children could claim it as their own, untwisted by silence or shame.

Chapter 48

LOVE NEEDS WITNESSES

Love has to be shown so it can be believed.

Luke's high school graduation baked under an early-summer sun.

Sophia cried through every speech.

Lila whooped too loudly when her brother's name was called.

Nathan watched, feeling something settle inside him. For so long, he'd loved people quietly, convinced the feeling alone was enough. But Sophia had taught him otherwise.

Love has to be shown so it can be believed. Kisses at the door. Notes tucked into lunches. Music drifting down hallways at bedtime. Apologies in the kitchen, sleeves rolled up. Fingertips intertwined in the supermarket line. Showing up…and showing up again.

He realized that, when his children stood where he stood now, they would remember not the flawless days, but the moments love stepped out into the open and let itself be seen.

Chapter 49

NIGHT SONGS

Sleep, when it came, felt like permission.

Nathan used to imagine healing as a dramatic arrival—rain breaking open a heavy sky. Instead, it crept in on soft feet, moments so small they were almost invisible.

Some nights, he woke and found Sophia asleep beside him, her breathing deep and even. He would slip from the bed, padding through the dim house, fingertips grazing the backs of chairs, checking that windows were locked. The old reflexes didn't disappear; they lingered like a familiar refrain.

In the kitchen's quiet, he would lean a hand against the counter and understand just how much fear had once run his life. The teenage boy who believed that perfection, silence, invisibility might keep him safe—that boy still lived inside him, but Nathan was learning to give him rest.

If he startled at a slammed door, a loud sound from the street, or lay awake until 3:00 a.m., it didn't mean he was broken. It only meant he was human, still here.

Sleep, when it came, felt like permission.

Chapter 50

THE LANGUAGE OF TOUCH

You're safe here. I mean no harm.

When Lila was small, she'd climb him like a tree—hands, sticky from fruit snacks, tugging his ears, patting his beard. With Luke, touch started differently: a hesitant lean, the gentle resting of a head against Nathan's knee during a movie.

Richard had rewired Nathan's sense of physical contact, turned it into something to brace against. It took years to relearn that touch could be sanctuary, not control.

He promised himself his kids would never wonder if an embrace was safe. He wouldn't force it, but he would always offer.

And over the years, affection built itself in small, unremarkable moments—a hand on a back bent over homework, fingers rustling hair after a long day, strong arms wrapping around a shaking frame after bad news. Thousands of touches saying, *You're safe here. I mean no harm.*

Chapter 51

THE GIFT OF BOREDOM

To believe boredom could be, not a void,
but a shelter.

After Richard, Nathan's brain still craved spikes of adrenaline. Peace felt alien, boredom a warning.

Fatherhood slowed him. Afternoons watching Lila blow soap bubbles until the wand dripped, listening to Luke plunk out uneven scales for the hundredth time. Saturdays running errands, slapping together pancakes, playing board games that trailed off into laughter.

He learned to unclench into the quiet. To let the urge for "what's next?" dissolve into *"this is enough."* To believe boredom could be, not a void, but a shelter.

Chapter 52

THE LIE OF SELF-SUFFICIENCY

**"We're built to need each other.
That's not shameful—that's the best thing
about being human."**

As a teenager, Nathan learned to carry everyone's weight—his wounds, his mother's burdens—certain that needing help was weakness.

Sophia dismantled that belief with quiet persistence. She asked plainly for what she needed. She accepted apologies without suspicion.

It took years, but he began to see that true strength was trusting someone to take some of your load. That calling Angela just to say, *"I miss you,"* was not indulgence but connection. That saying, *"I'm not okay,"* to Sophia didn't make him less of a partner; it made them more of a team.

When Luke once tried, alone, to tough out a problem at school, Nathan told him, "We're built to need each other. That's not shameful—that's the best thing about being human."

Chapter 53

RUINS AND RECONSTRUCTIONS

Triggers hid everywhere.

Triggers hid everywhere—in a voice raised at the grocery store, a slammed door two rooms away. When his kids were young, old rage could ambush him out of nowhere.

Unlike Richard, he refused to turn it into a weapon. The first step was naming it: *I'm really mad right now, but I'm not going to yell.*

Sometimes he left the room until he could breathe without shaking. Every time calm returned, the ground under them solidified. He saw it in their eyes—the belief that a storm could pass without wreckage, that rebuilding was possible.

And in quiet moments afterward, when a small voice would say, "It's okay, Dad," with an arm around his waist, Nathan knew that breaking the cycle wasn't a single act. It was choosing repair over destruction, again and again.

Chapter 54

WHEN LOVE IS WORK

Love can be loud or soft, but it is always the decision to stay.

Love, he learned, wasn't a feeling you rode like a current. It was work—patient, repetitive, exhausting in seasons, and luminous in others.

The autumn both kids turned prickly, Lila's sharp words and slammed doors braided with Luke's quiet withdrawals from family meals.

It was too easy to hear accusation in the silence. Sophia's voice steadied him. "They'll come back. Keep showing up."

So he ferried them to practices without filling the air. Set dinner on the table even if they took plates to their rooms. Left notes instead of lectures.

On the other side, they came back—in jokes tossed across the couch, in late-night talks that stepped gently into trust again.

Love can be loud or soft, but it is always the decision to stay.

Chapter 55

KINDNESS AS A LEGACY

What had been done to him would not be done through him. And that was victory enough.

If cruelty could ripple outward for decades, so could kindness. Nathan saw it in Luke, the boy who spotted the lonely kid on the playground and invited him over. In Lila, who stopped to defend classmates everyone else ignored. In Sophia, who reminded the people she loved to rest as she refilled their tea.

He began to believe that his truest legacy wasn't survival; it was what survival allowed him to create—a chain of tenderness that stretched beyond their walls.

What had been done *to* him would not be done *through* him. And that was victory enough.

Chapter 56

SEASONS OF FORGIVENESS

Letting go became an act of radical self-love...
and a path toward the peace he'd once thought
was reserved for other people.

Forgiveness, for Nathan, was a journey, not a one-time decision. Early on, he tried to forgive Richard, if only to quiet his own mind. But it remained impossible, a jagged edge always catching in his heart.

Over the years, he realized that forgiveness wasn't about Richard at all. It was about setting down his own burden—the anger, the urge to punish, the fear of repayment. It meant refusing to let the past dictate his future or steal his joy.

Some acts he could never approve, never absolve. But as he let go of the expectation that the past would be made right, he found he had more energy for the present, more gentleness for his children and himself.

He told this to Luke once, after a friendship ended in betrayal: "Forgiveness doesn't mean everything's okay. It means *you're okay*, even if the person who hurt you never is."

Letting go became an act of radical self-love...and a path toward the peace he'd once thought was reserved for other people.

Chapter 57

QUESTIONS WITHOUT END

Why did it happen to us? Why didn't we leave
sooner? Why didn't anyone rescue us?
Why was Mother—my hero—so powerless?

Some pain lingers in the body, but most takes root in the mind. For Nathan, the years after Richard felt as if he were being haunted by invisible hands—not only the memory of what had happened, but staggering, impossible question: *Why did it happen to us? Why didn't we leave sooner? Why didn't anyone rescue us? Why was Mother—my hero—so powerless?*

These questions had no real answers. But adulthood gave him room to sit with them, uncomfortable as they were.

One night, when Luke was home from college, they sat on the porch just after a summer rain. The trees sparkled. Nathan found himself saying, "I used to think healing meant finding answers. But, some things, we'll never know why. All we can do is decide what comes next."

Luke nodded, then asked, "Did you ever forgive him?"

Nathan was silent a while. "No. Not in the way people mean. What I learned to do was forgive myself—my mistakes, my need for help, even my anger. I stopped expecting the past to behave differently. That was enough."

With every retelling, the edges softened. Not the reality, but his relationship to it. He learned, slowly, that generational pain could end—not by pretending the past didn't matter, but by refusing to let it control the future.

That became his vow, his North Star, as he moved deeper into parenthood: Face every ache, and keep building anyway.

Chapter 58

THE MANY LANGUAGES OF LOVE

He learned to notice, to name,
to make love visible and tangible

Nathan approached love the way he first learned to survive: quietly, fiercely, silently. Over the years, Sophia showed him there are many ways to show love—some loud, some soft, and not all the ways look like the ones you grew up with.

For Sophia, love wasn't just words at bedtime or comfort after tears. It was planning a surprise dinner, running errands so he could rest, buying his favorite snacks, defending him during awkward family visits, reminding him to call Angela even when he resisted.

Lila often showed love with humor, Luke with shy touches, Mei with steady letters year after year.

Nathan realized that in his family, love was fluid—sometimes a hug, sometimes a hard truth, sometimes the simple act of not giving up.

He began to ask, "What does love look like for you?" and let his family answer. Lila with late-night talks, Luke by sharing music, Sophia by showing up, again and again, no matter his moods.

He learned to notice, to name, to make love visible and tangible. This was how his children learned too—not just to feel loved, but to see it, give it, and hold it as their own.

Chapter 59

KEEPING VIGIL

He offered it now, over and over,
in every small way he could.

Later in life, Nathan realized how little control we truly have—not just over the world, but even over the people we treasure most. The only choice is to bear witness: to keep vigil at the edges of another's pain, to promise not to look away.

When Lila's best friend's parents divorced, she came home weeping, convinced nothing would ever feel certain again. When Luke came out as bi in high school, Nathan listened as his son spoke about fear and bullying; he didn't pretend to understand perfectly, but he promised never to flinch.

Nathan learned that the truest form of support was not advice, platitudes, or distractions—but simply remaining. Camping out in the overwhelmingness, offering presence, trusting that showing up is sometimes the only answer.

The wordless nights, the steady arm around a shaking shoulder, the vow: "You're not alone. I'm not leaving." That, he realized, was what his own younger self most needed.

He offered it now, over and over, in every small way he could.

Chapter 60

SHOWING UP FOR THE LONG GAME

Years of surviving Richard left Nathan with an intolerance for uncertainty. He wanted his children to be happy *now*, safe *now*, healed *now*. But life, he learned, is gradual—a slow layering of failure and success, days that seem pointless until, abruptly, everything changes.

He saw it as Lila grew bold, then shy, then bold again. As Luke stumbled in academics, then flourished in music. As his own wounds healed and reopened, sometimes on the very same day.

He learned to respect the slow arc of becoming. To coach soccer or fold laundry or scrub out the basement, trusting that all the small things accumulate into something whole.

Sophia called this "showing up for the long game." He came to believe it's all anyone can do.

Chapter 61

THE GEOMETRY OF FAMILY

*His greatest lesson was seeing how love, choice,
and history melded
into something richer.*

Nathan thought for a long time that family was defined by DNA. His greatest lesson was seeing how love, choice, and history melded into something richer.

Family, he learned, is not a straight line. It's a web—a series of intersections, threads, and knots. Birth parents, adoptive parents, found siblings, beloved friends—each person adding their own pattern.

When Luke struggled with belonging in college, Nathan told him, "Blood matters, but not more than time spent, care given, trust earned. Family is anybody who stays, who helps you be your best."

In that way, Nathan found peace with his own complicated history: the deep bond with Angela, the heartbreaking loss, and the bright new ties to Sophia, Lila, Luke, and even, in some way, Mei.

The shape of his family symbolized what he valued—endurance, compassion, honesty. He taught his children to claim the same right: to make, and remake, what family means.

Chapter 62

SAVORING JOY

"You're not betraying anyone by celebrating."

For a survivor, happiness can feel both foreign and fleeting—as if by lingering on it, you might curse it. Nathan's big parenting shift came when he learned to let joy last.

Sometimes, it was the little things: coffee with Sophia before sunrise, Luke's piano playing drifting up the stairs, Lila's shrieking laughter at a ridiculous meme.

But, sometimes, it was public, unignorable—the pride he felt when Luke got accepted to college, when Lila won her first writing prize, when Sophia's nonprofit raised a record amount in one month.

Survivors are trained by trauma to seek the exits—to anticipate disaster. Nathan taught himself, and then his kids, to sit in the center of the good a little longer. Take photos. Make a fuss. Let yourself believe you deserve it, even just for tonight.

"It's not wrong to be happy," he told Luke one Christmas Eve. "You're not betraying anyone by celebrating."

Chapter 63

THE NECESSITY OF SILENCE

After so many years of tension, Nathan learned to appreciate silence.

After so many years of tension, Nathan learned to appreciate silence—not the fear-filled hush of his childhood home, but the chosen quiet of peace.

He found it in early-morning walks, in silent reading by the window, in the hush that settled over the house after the kids had gone out.

Silence, he saw now, was not an absence but a richness—a chance to reflect, to dream, to remember. In silence, he could feel the subtle healing of years; the nerves that once screamed in anticipation of harm were now at rest, humming gently, expecting only calm.

He learned to teach his children the same: how to find their own quiet. How to carve out space for thought, for rest, for simply being. It was in these silent moments that Nathan felt most certain he had built a new life on purpose, not just in reaction to the old one.

Chapter 64

WRESTLING WITH FAITH

*Trauma had made it hard for Nathan to believe
in much of anything—
God, luck, happy endings.*

Trauma had made it hard for Nathan to believe in much of anything—God, luck, happy endings. He'd lived too long waiting for the other shoe to drop.

But in adulthood, as Sophia's faith flickered and changed, and as the kids found their own paths, Nathan allowed a gentler kind of belief to return—not religious, but rooted in hope and in the mystery of survival.

He came to trust in the possibility of good's return. In forgiveness, in the capacity to change, in the cycle of broken things becoming beautiful through attention and care.

Close friends would call him pessimistic; he'd smile and correct them. "Not pessimistic. Just experienced. But what amazes me is how good the world can still be—even after everything."

Chapter 65

THE GIFT OF LETTING GO

No parent escapes regret.

No parent escapes regret. Nathan spent too many years believing that hope was dangerous, that leftover scars made him a bad example, that he had to save his children from every possible hurt.

With time, he learned to let go. Not of love, nor responsibility, but of the fantasy that he could engineer perfection.

He let go of measuring himself against others' lives, of believing his worth was measured in milestones or adherence to a "normal" ideal.

He let Lila choose a college states away, let Luke chase not security but joy, let Sophia push her career further than he'd ever imagined. He learned to say goodbye when necessary, to trust in their return.

Letting go wasn't loss, but the truest expression of faith—in those he loved, and in the world they had built together.

Chapter 66

UNMAKING THE OLD STORY

*He would never be able to change
the past or what happened in it.*

As the kids grew and the house emptied, Nathan found himself reflecting—sometimes in the solitude of his study, sometimes while pulling weeds in the backyard—on the story he'd once believed about himself.

For so long, survival had been about shrinking: making himself small, hoping to dodge Richard's attention, trying not to take up space or make waves. Back then, survival and silence were synonyms. Old wounds taught him to anticipate disappointment, believe he was trouble, and expect abandonment. Even years removed from that storm, those lessons lingered.

But when the house was still—when silence meant comfort, not warning—he realized healing meant writing a new story. Not erasing the past, but rewriting what came after.

Instead of shrinking, he learned to root. To remain even when uncomfortable. To say, "This is my home," out loud, in a voice that grew steadier every year.

Instead of vanishing, he showed up—for soccer games, airport pickups, long phone calls during hard freshman years, dinners in noisy restaurants where laughter spilled out too loud to go unnoticed.

Instead of assuming love was fleeting, he learned that love—daily, mundane, relentless—could be built, brick by brick, decision by decision.

Nathan became a gardener of rituals: packing sandwiches no matter how old his kids became, sending check-in texts every Sunday, making pancakes and bad dad jokes whenever someone needed to know they were wanted. Every ritual a remaking. Every "I love you" a contradiction to the old silence.

He would never be able to change the past or what happened in it. But he could unmake its echo, so his story—and his children's—was not about absence, but presence.

Chapter 67

TENDING ROOTS

Nathan learned to believe her.

When Luke came home for his first winter break, Nathan marveled at how much the boy—now a young man—still needed his old bed, his favorite mug, the weird painting Sophia hung in the front hall as a joke.

They all needed the roots.

Nathan realized that his deepest longing, as a child, had not just been for safety, but for a feeling of belonging—of having a place in a home that would not disappear.

He became intentional about tending those roots. He welcomed Lila's friends as extensions of his family. He printed and framed family pictures—even the blurry, silly ones—so his children saw themselves woven into their home's very walls.

On holidays, he told the stories of their childhoods and his own—not to dwell on fear, but to highlight the chain of survival. "We came through a lot," he'd say, "but look who we are now."

If his children forgot to water their roots—if they drifted, wobbled, became untethered—he reminded them that it takes time to grow steady, and that coming home (in any sense) was a win, not a regression.

Sophia, quieter in her wisdom, said it best one night: "We never outgrow the need for a place to be welcome exactly as we are. We just get to name that place ourselves."

Nathan learned to believe her.

Chapter 68

LET THE WORLD IN

The hardest habit to unlearn was isolation.

The hardest habit to unlearn was isolation. For years, Nathan's instinct in crisis was to close ranks: retreat, hide, avoid. Vulnerability seemed dangerous.

But then he noticed the more he opened the door—literally and metaphorically—to other people, the happier his world became.

He grew close to Sophia's family, even the complicated members. He made peace, slowly, with his own mother, forgiving her for her silences and for the choices she'd made when she was at her weakest. He let himself care about neighbors, musicians he met in local bars, kids from his nonprofit who stayed late just to talk.

He discovered that intimacy is not about never being betrayed but about repeatedly saying, "In this space, in this moment, you are safe." And the more he offered that safety, the richer his life grew.

Lila once told him, after a particularly long kitchen-table conversation, "Dad, we're lucky—we know how to talk through anything."

Nathan smiled, thinking of the decades it had taken for him to learn to talk about anything at all.

Chapter 69

THE FAMILY WE MAKE

Nathan became more convinced than ever that
'family' is an act, a verb, not a noun.

As the pages of family life filled with scribbled notes—letters from Mei, postcards from Lila's travels, programs from Luke's recitals—Nathan became more convinced than ever that "family" is an act, a verb, not a noun.

He realized how many people in his children's orbit longed for homes as inclusive as theirs: kids whose parents were missing or distracted, partners who'd never known gentle love, friends who only ever saw family as a place of leaving, not returning.

So he made it a mission—in deliberate, daily ways—to invite people in. Dinner tables were set with extra places. Thanksgiving meant as many as wanted could come, and sometimes random acquaintances showed up, grateful to have a place that didn't judge, didn't question, only offered kindness.

At first, he did this for his children, afraid they'd someday feel rootless, as he once had. But in time he saw that he was healing himself too. Every meal, every new story shared around their battered kitchen table was a welcome home.

Chapter 70

THE LETTERS WE'LL LEAVE BEHIND

*Some truths—about survival, forgiveness,
hope—took time to sink in.*

Nathan kept every letter Mei sent, every essay Lila wrote, every heartfelt card Luke scribbled from college. It started as a way to honor their journeys, but over time it became something more: a record, a reminder, a legacy.

As he aged, Nathan understood that not all wisdom could be spoken aloud. Some truths—about survival, forgiveness, hope—took time to sink in. Some needed to be found and rediscovered at the right moment.

So he began to write his own letters. Some he mailed; many he left unsealed in a box for his children to find someday: lessons he couldn't always say in person, confessions of worry and pride, instructions not for the tasks of life but for its heart.

He wrote to Lila: "Don't be embarrassed to be gentle. The world needs it more than you know."

To Luke: "There will be days you want to disappear. Don't. Let yourself be found."

To Sophia, on an anniversary: "You saved me, not by fixing my wounds but by letting me be honest about them."

He wrote until the ink ran out, certain that when the kids found these someday, they would know everything that mattered: They were chosen, wanted, and believed in. Softness is strength. Families aren't made—they are built.

Chapter 71

THE LIGHT, NOT THE CHAIN

"You taught us how to reclaim the sun."

On his last birthday before retirement, Nathan woke to a card on his pillow: a photograph of the four of them at the beach, waves crashing behind, everyone laughing, hair windblown and faces sunstruck.

On the back, Lila had written, "You taught us how to reclaim the sun."

It made him cry over his pancakes, in the quiet kitchen before anyone else was up. For so long, his life had been about breaking chains—refusing to carry forward the hurt he'd grown up with. But now, in his gentle, brightly lit home, he realized it isn't enough to break chains. You have to choose what to grow in their place.

Nathan had learned to build his family around the light— trust, apologies, laughter, presence. And in doing that, he'd given his children something better than safety—freedom.

Chapter 72

FULL CIRCLE

It felt, finally, like a completed circle.

Years after the threat was gone, after Richard was just a dark chapter and not a living specter, Nathan sometimes walked the old neighborhood, now gentrified and green. On certain summer evenings, he'd find himself standing outside his childhood house, or by the park where he once hid out to avoid going home, or on the street where he'd first found music offered a voice when silence was too heavy. He would linger, remembering the scared boy, the silent mother, and the menacing shadow that once filled every space.

But then he'd see the future in his mind—the home he'd made, the resilient love that grew from hard soil, the laughter that now belonged to his children's children.

It felt, finally, like a completed circle. The story wasn't just about endurance, but about choosing to be more than what happened to him. The house was only a house now. The ghosts were replaced by new music.

Wherever he went, Nathan carried the invisible map of all he'd survived, but also—finally—of all he called home.

Chapter 73

WHAT ENDURES

*He hoped they'd remember him as the father
who made them feel safe, seen, chosen, brave.*

At the end, Nathan hoped his kids wouldn't remember how perfect or imperfect he was as a parent. He hoped they'd remember him as the father who made them feel safe, seen, chosen, brave.

He hoped they'd remember the way he made mistakes and said sorry, the songs he sang off-key, the way he listened, really listened, when life fell apart.

He hoped they'd carry on the rituals of forgiveness and light he'd worked so long to grow. He hoped, in their own uncertain lives, they would choose—over and over—to be gentle, honest, and unafraid to love.

He'd learned, after so many years of survival, the lesson that truly endures is not how to escape fear or how to win against the darkness. It is how to bring your heart, stubbornly and with hope, to every table, every quiet hour...and to keep making a home of your own.

Chapter 74

THE EDGE OF SILENCE

"What does forgiveness feel like...really?"

Nathan Parker never pictured himself back in the old house, yet here he was—alone on the porch, the same midnight-blue paint chipping under his fingers. In the golden dusk of early autumn, the world felt full, demanding, expectant. It was the hush before something broke, the pause before a reckoning.

The wind played in the tall grass. Somewhere inside, Lila's laughter spilled out the front window, soft and broken by distance—the laughter of womanhood, not the giggle of a child. Luke's voice followed, lower now, brightening for guests, his piano fingers idly tapping some unseen rhythm on the banister.

Sophia had reorganized the kitchen only that morning, but every drawer Nathan opened still revealed their patterns— scuffed measuring cups, a chipped mug, the faint trace of crayon on the painted wood. Years ago, these familiar objects had tethered him when he was adrift. Now, they felt like punctuation: the end of one long sentence, the beginning of something unnamed.

Angela's last letter sat folded in his jacket pocket, edges worn bright by decades of rereading. "Remember, Nathan, pain doesn't get the last word," she wrote. "You decide what comes after."

For the first time in months, the house was full. Lila was home from the city, Luke down from his university. Even Mei was staying over, a rare convergence that felt both impossible and essential. They had promised one another a weekend with no distractions: no screens, no schedules, just food and old stories and the gentle, deliberate practice of kin.

Nathan stepped in from the porch, shut the door against the cooling night, and let laughter draw him to the living room. They sat, scattered and sprawled across furniture, sharing the old afghan Angela knitted when he was still in grade school. Mei perched quietly at one end, her smile gentle, eyes roving the room as if to memorize every detail.

Stories flowed—mostly Lila's, her hands carving wild arcs through the air, memories spinning from childhood until laughter stilled the room. Even Sophia was giddy, face flushed with something halfway between nostalgia and disbelief.

But after dinner—when the candles flickered low, and the air grew heavy—Luke's gaze found Nathan. "Dad," he asked, "what does forgiveness feel like…really?"

Nathan's breath caught. *How do I answer a question I'm still learning?* he thought, feeling both humbled and strangely honored by his son's trust.

The room stilled.

Nathan traced a glass ring on the coffee table, considering how to answer this question after a lifetime of wrestling with ghosts.

Finally, he spoke softly. "It's like any wound that heals slowly. There's always a scar. Some days, you hardly notice it; other days, it aches. Forgiveness isn't about forgetting or pretending it didn't hurt. It's deciding—again and again—that the pain won't decide who you are or how you love back."

Mei's eyes glistened. Lila bit her lip, glancing at Sophia, who nodded almost imperceptibly.

"There's more?" Luke pressed.

Nathan met his son's gaze. "Sometimes, forgiveness is for yourself—letting go of the burden so you don't pass it on."

He didn't mention Richard by name, but everyone in the room felt his shape in the words. The man who had tried, and failed, to make Nathan small. The man whose violence once ruled every heartbeat in this house. The man who had shaped their story by his absence as much as by his presence.

Angela's words echoed again. *You decide what comes after.*

Dishes done, the family drifted to routines: Lila and Sophia vanished upstairs to sort old photographs, voices rising in laughter. Luke settled at the ancient piano, coaxing gentle chords from the warped keys, while Mei leaned on the farthest arm of the sofa, seemingly content just to watch the scene unfold.

Nathan slipped to the back porch, the weight of memory and gratitude heavy and aching in his chest. The air crackled with the edge of an oncoming storm, the kind that once filled him with dread, but now with something close to anticipation.

He realized he was not afraid of storms anymore.

He was halfway through Angela's old letter, the ink nearly faded, when a car's headlights swept the driveway—two quick flashes, then darkness.

Nathan tensed. Old habits die hard—the surge of adrenaline, the bracing for bad news.

But the car didn't approach. It idled by the curb, a figure sitting motionless behind the wheel.

Minutes passed, marked only by the sound of the wind and vague thunder rolling in the distance. Nathan waited, senses on high alert—an instinct honed by years of living on the edge of other people's rage.

Then, as quickly as it arrived, the car pulled away. No voices, no confrontation. Just a silent visitor, gone as suddenly as it appeared.

But as Nathan stood to go inside, he saw it: an envelope, pale against the black wood of the porch steps.

He knelt, heart hammering, and picked it up. There was no name on the front, only a single initial in sharp, hurried script: *R.*

Chapter 75

THE LETTER

I am sorry.

Nathan sat on the edge of the porch, hands shaking so hard the letter almost slipped away. He stared at the envelope, torn between dread and curiosity—between a fear he thought he'd outgrown and a terrible need to know. The single initial—*R*—scrawled across the front made his stomach drop.

Of course, it would never be his full name; even in apology, Richard stays hidden.

A crack of thunder startled him, but he tore open the envelope before he could talk himself out of it.

Inside was a single sheet of heavyweight paper and a photograph—grainy, black-and-white, unmistakably old. Nathan recognized himself at sixteen: thin, grim, trapped between Richard and Angela on the front steps of this very house as Richard's hand gripped Nathan's shoulder, his expression unreadable.

The letter was brief:

Nathan,

After all these years, I owe you more than this—more than I will ever be able to say in a letter. Perhaps

I never knew how to love, or to stop myself from the harm I caused. I have watched you, from a distance, build the life I could never understand. If there is any mercy left in you, make sure you don't become me. Let the next generation live free.

I am sorry.

—R.

Nathan lingered on the porch, rain drumming a steady rhythm as the old photograph slipped between his fingers. Remorse or manipulation? It didn't matter—there was no erasing what had been.

The silence around him thickened, but within a quiet resolve stirred. This story was far from over, and the next chapter was his to write.

He thought of all the warnings—about generational curses, about the violence that trickles down, about the children of abusers becoming abusers themselves if they weren't vigilant, weren't open, weren't forgiving.

He realized Richard was alive. Watching from somewhere far off, sending this letter not for reunion or redemption, but as a warning, an admission, a final urge to sever the chain for good.

As rain pounded the roof in a relentless drumbeat, Nathan closed his eyes, feeling the wild storm outside echo a rare sense of absolution—no longer fear, but a fierce claim on what came next.

Nathan stepped inside, closing the door against the storm. With the letter still damp in his hand, he felt both disturbed and strangely free. *Nathan folded the letter carefully, rain dampening the edges as if it were the tears he refused to shed. The storm's first drops had kissed his skin, but inside a quiet resolve settled.*

No more shadows. No more silence. I decide what comes next.

Mei had joined Luke by the window as Sophia and Lila thumped down the stairs, all of them caught mid-conversation.

He held the open envelope in his outstretched hand and in a quiet voice said, "I...just found this."

The room fell instantly silent.

Lila spoke first, her voice small. "Is it over, Dad?"

Nathan shook his head, unable to answer...because the truth was, in families like theirs, the past is never just the past. It lingers. It returns. Or it asks, again and again, to be rewritten.

Rain battered the windows as they reopened the letter together. The old black-and-white picture sat between them, demanding its own reckoning.

None of them spoke. Outside, the car was gone. But its shadow clung to the curve of the street, as if a single visitor could push Reset on everything they had believed was settled.

And in that moment, Nathan understood: The most dangerous stories are never those that end, but the ones left unfinished.

Would the cycle close, or would it return—one day, years from now—in ways they could never imagine?

Nathan glanced at his family—at Mei's haunted gaze, Sophia's strength, Luke's wary hope, Lila's fear and ferocity.

Storm light flashed beyond the windows.

For a heartbeat, the house was silent; then thunder rolled, urging them all forward, step by uncertain step, into whatever future waited beyond the edge of silence.

Through resilience, Nathan found his strength. At last, he broke the chains.

National Domestic Violence Hotline: 1-800-799-7233

1 in 4 Men Crisis Line: 1-800-884-4357

Your voice matters.

Your healing is possible.

You are not alone.

If you or someone you know is experiencing domestic violence, please reach out for help. Resources are available for all survivors, regardless of gender. Your safety and healing matter.

For those inspired by Nathan's story: Consider supporting organizations that provide services to male domestic violence survivors, advocate for gender-inclusive policies, and help create a world where all victims are believed and supported.

A LETTER FROM THE AUTHOR

Dear Reader,

If you have made it to this page, you have already traveled through shadow and light. You've felt the cracks in the walls; the slam of doors meant to keep you out, or in; the long nights when silence felt heavier than sound; and the slow, aching climb toward something like freedom. You've witnessed Nathan's story. But woven through his journey are truths that feel as old as memory itself, the kind that settle deep and never let go. His fight is not only his; it belongs to so many who have been told their pain is too small or too inconvenient to name.

Writing *Resilience: Breaking the Chains* was similar to walking barefoot through glass. Every word asked a question: Will you tell it as it is, even if your hands shake? Will you open the door to places long kept locked? Will you risk being truly seen? Again and again, the answer was yes. Because silence grows in the dark, and shame feeds on silence. And breaking those chains always begins with a single voice saying, *"Enough."*

If you've ever been told to toughen up, to get over it, or to bury your pain so deep no one can find it, let these pages be my hand reaching for yours. If you've ever been made to feel invisible, let this be your reminder: I see you. I believe you. And you are not alone.

I hope, as you close this book, you carry something with you—courage, perhaps. Or the small, steady belief that healing is possible, even when it doesn't look the way you imagined. That it's okay to move forward slowly, to stumble, to stop and start again. *Forward is still forward.*

Because resilience has never been about standing tall without falling. It's about getting back up, no matter how many times the world has knocked you down.

If you've made it here, thank you for listening, for holding this story, and for letting it live beside your own. Stories like this are not easy to tell, and they are not easy to hear, but they matter because they remind us that survival is not the end of the journey; healing is. My hope is that somewhere in these pages, you found a piece of truth that feels like your own... and the courage to carry it forward.

With gratitude and solidarity,

Eugene Z. Bertrand

ACKNOWLEDGMENTS

This book would not exist without the encouragement and support I have received throughout this journey. My gratitude goes to every survivor who faces each day with courage and to those who strive to break unspoken cycles and heal; your strength was the heartbeat behind every word.

Thank you to my editorial team and the entire staff at Halo for your exceptional care, guidance, and dedication—you helped me find my voice and shape it with clarity.

LET'S CONNECT

LinkedIn: https://www.linkedin.com/in/eugene-bertrand

Website: https://eugenezbertrand.com